My God, My God

My God, My God

Is It Possible to Believe Anymore?

MICHAEL P. JENSEN

CASCADE *Books* · Eugene, Oregon

MY GOD, MY GOD
Is It Possible to Believe Anymore?

Copyright © 2013 Michael P. Jensen. All rights reserved. Except for brief quotations in critical publications or reviews, no part of this book may be reproduced in any manner without prior written permission from the publisher. Write: Permissions. Wipf and Stock Publishers, 199 W. 8th Ave., Suite 3, Eugene, OR 97401.

Cascade Books
An Imprint of Wipf and Stock Publishers
199 W. 8th Ave., Suite 3
Eugene, OR 97401

www.wipfandstock.com

ISBN 13: 978-1-62032-552-0

Cataloguing-in-Publication Data:

Jensen, Michael P.

My God, my God : is it possible to believe anymore? / Michael P. Jensen.

viii + 110 p. ; 23 cm. Includes bibliographical references and indexes.

ISBN 13: 978-1-62032-552-0

1. Apologetics. 2. Atheism—History. 3. Civilization—Western. I. Title.

BT1102 .J37 2013

Manufactured in the U.S.A.

To Simon, Sacha, Matilda, Freya, Charlie, and Maggie

Contents

ONE

Believe It, or Not

. . . I think that I still have some sort of faith or something. But I can't really pinpoint what that means at this point in time.

SARAH BLASKO, *MUSICIAN*

I BELIEVING NOW AND THEN

What does it take for a person to have a faith in God in the twenty-first century?

What you are about to read is an attempt to answer this most personal, and for many people most pressing, of questions. But we need to be aware of the context in which this wrestle to believe takes place. Most of us are, at least vaguely, aware that having a religious faith has not been as complex a matter at other points in history as it is today. Some would even argue that to own up to a faith in a deity of any kind is to admit to a kind of intellectual and personal dishonesty. For others, such as the Australian musician Sarah Blasko (1976–), who grew up as the child of evangelical missionaries, faith is still there but somehow indefinable and distant.[1]

1. Blasko, "Asking Sarah Blasko."

1

Is "faith"—whatever that is—even possible anymore?

Once upon a time, it was not so difficult to believe. Believing in God was like breathing. It was a second sense of which people were hardly aware. Even with a man as rational as the great English philosopher John Locke (1632–1704) in the seventeenth century, lack of religious belief was an extraordinary and aberrant thing that wasn't worth tolerating because it must surely lead to social chaos and even treasonable behavior. Philosophers like the great medieval thinkers Anselm of Canterbury (1033–1109) and Thomas Aquinas (1225–74) offered their famous arguments for the existence of God not because they imagined that they would convince a non-believer but because they saw them as confirming what believers (that is, *everybody*) knew to be already true.

Not only was the world self-evidently the handiwork of the Creator, but it was also the case that it was shot through with his divinity. Divinity oozed from physicality. You could pick up a handful of earth and feel that it had more to it than the solid: that it had in it some *spirit*. And that was because the dirt crumbling in your fingers and sticking underneath your fingernails was a link, however small, in a great chain of being that had its anchor point on the highest being—namely, God. Human beings too, for all their earthiness, were a part of this great connected whole in which they could actively participate through prayers and other religious acts, mediated through the agency of the church. The "divine" and the "natural" were not separate explanations for the workings of the world.

Today we like to think of believing, as we like to think of many things, as primarily a choice. We think of our religious views as a preference—not a trivial one, it should be granted, but a preference nonetheless. It's highly personal, as most choices are. What's more, believing in God has become a highly contested choice, vehemently challenged by some of the most prominent intellectuals of our times.

How has this come about? It would be too easy to say that the rise of the scientific worldview is the culprit. That is a common way of telling the story: as science and technology have enabled us to grasp the world more successfully and efficiently, the less mysterious the world has seemed. Take medicine, for example: once we could talk about bacteria and viruses and their effects, we could start addressing illnesses without supposing that a priest—or a witch—is going to have a great deal to contribute either way. It is true that science has provided alternative explanations of the workings of the world that at many points make it apparently unnecessary to appeal to a divine power. But that would be to miss the story of how the scientific worldview come to prominence in the first place; and how it depended for its emergence on certain changes in the way faith and belief were thought of in Western Europe. The scientific worldview did not *cause* the change in the nature of believing, since it arose at the same time as the changes themselves took place.

That change had to do with the extraordinary movement within Western Christianity: the Reformation of the sixteenth century. The Reformation was a revolution in the idea of faith itself.[2] It took the central notion of "faith" to mean not merely "believing certain propositions to be true and others to be false" but the giving of the whole of one's self in deep trust to the promises of God. This idea was not entirely novel, but the emphasis put upon it by thinkers like the great Reformer Martin Luther (1483–1546) certainly was. The big thing that connected you to the divine world was now an inward and individual matter, whereas before this the external work of baptism was held to be the ground of your religious life. And this believing, this faith, was part of your life's story: it was now possible to tell a story of not believing and *then* believing, of coming to know what trust in the promises of God was as the Spirit of God did its work on you and you changed. Though the Reformers were adamant that faith itself was a work of God in the human person, it was still the case that the human person's will, reason, and affections were involved in the getting of faith. Even if one ought retrospectively to speak of the illumination of God's Holy Spirit working in your heart to bring faith to flame, the experience of coming to faith felt certainly as if it involved one's hearing, understanding, and a moment of decision. At this point, faith became an act of the will—a reality decided upon. It is mine to choose; and mine to reject.

Instead of seeing God's presence rippling through nature, the Reformers warned of the danger of confusing the created things with the Creator himself. They saw—or rather, heard—God's voice in the Bible, the Word of God. This was God's powerful and singular instrument to work on the human heart. And you didn't have to perform gymnastics of interpretation to hear it. To look elsewhere was to miss the point—to stop up one's ears to the saving message of God's love.

---

2. I am aware that I have zeroed in on what is in many ways a record of an inglorious division between Christians, Protestant and Catholic. But the impact of this revolution in faith was felt on both sides of the divide.

But this shift in outlook was extraordinary because it actually empowered the investigation of the world. Peter Harrison (1955–), Research Professor at the University of Queensland and a Senior Research Fellow at the Ian Ramsay Centre in Oxford, writes:

> . . . the idea, first proposed in the seventeenth century, that nature was governed by mathematical laws, was directly informed by theological considerations. The move towards offering mechanical explanations in physics also owed much to a particular religious perspective. The adoption of more literal approaches to the interpretation of the Bible, usually assumed to have been an impediment to science, also had an important, if indirect, role in these developments, promoting a non-symbolic and utilitarian understanding of the natural world which was conducive to the scientific approach.[3]

If anything, the leading theologians of the Protestant movement were keen to emphasize the sheer transcendent otherness of God—his separateness from the world. If anything, the gospel of the bleeding and dying Jesus Christ revealed to humankind the radical alienation of humankind from the divine being. The significance of this separation of God from his creation was that the world's natural processes became available for study on their own terms, without the confusion of a metaphysical explanation. As Harrison argues, this was the beginning of the scientific revolution, and a revolution in the way people in the West thought about believing in God.

In turn, this new explanation of God is related to the world is crucial to understanding what people generally think themselves to be doing when they accept or reject religious faith in the twenty-first century. The story we most commonly tell ourselves is that religious faith is in rapid decline because scientific knowledge is increasing. And yet the picture is actually more complex. What lies at the heart of the story of belief during the time of post-Christian late modernity is in fact a piece of *theological* thinking about the nature of God's relationship to the world and the kind of thing human beings are doing when they say they believe—or don't believe—in a being like God.

3. Harrison, "Christianity and the Rise of Western Science."

II THE UNCHOOSEABLE CHOICE

But we need to pause here and retrace our steps somewhat, because there's a complication to the story—a complication I call the "unchooseable choice" condition. It is true that people today speak of belief in God as something that one chooses for oneself. But there's a contradiction here, too. People also characteristically speak of being religious or not as something about themselves that they can't change and that just "is"—like their eye color or race. They will say "I am not a religious person." Philosopher Alain de Botton (1969–) has spoken of his unbelief as if it was inescapable fact about him that was not at all open to revision or question regardless of any choice he might make:

> I cannot be sure why I am a non-believer exactly. Surely much does have to do with the way I was raised in a family of non-believers, and a rational outlook very much at the fore. So the key question for me isn't whether one should believe or not, but where one goes to—as an atheist—once the non-existence of God is clear.[4]

Religious beliefs, or the lack of them, are so deeply ingrained in us from childhood that we can close off a conversation about religious matters by simply referring to our particular upbringing. "I was raised a Presbyterian,"[5] for example, is what people say when they mean "I really don't want to talk about religion, thanks just the same." So, we have a choice that, ironically, many people feel they can't choose.

Scott Adams (1957–), author of the comic strip *Dilbert*, makes a perceptive comment about this on his blog.[6] He starts with the assertion that "research indicates that some people are born with a natural inclination for belief and some are not." He puts himself in the latter category: he's a born non-believer. He is certainly not opposed to religious belief and is even strongly positive about its benefits. Being religious is a very strong indicator of better health and a more satisfying life. He is even happy to consider his lack of ability to believe as something of a handicap. He just can't shake the impression that all of us (atheists or theists) are deluded about our grasp of "the real" or "the truth."

This condition is part of a deeper paradox at the heart of the culture of the West. It's a paradox which reverberates right through Western politics,

4. de Botton and Rosner, "Interview with Alain de Botton."

5. . . . or Catholic, or Orthodox, or Muslim, or C of E . . .

6. Adams, "Talent or Handicap."

science, economics, and education, and which has no obvious philosophical solution. It's this: on the one hand, we exalt the notion of human autonomous free will. It's a fine idea, all right: liberty is an aspiration which lends the human individual dignity and enables us to talk about the rights and duties we owe each other regardless of skin color or gender. The freedom to pursue happiness is the basis of our consumer economy, and of our system of justice, in which we hold individuals largely responsible for their actions as far as we can. We expect it from each other. And yet at the same time, various branches of human knowledge are offering powerful descriptions of the human condition as entirely and comprehensively determined by factors outside of our control—whether that be genes, natural selection, brain chemistry, our parents, or whatever else. So, the whole idea of free choice may turn out to be a grand illusion. That's certainly the argument of leading New Atheist Sam Harris (1967–) in his book *Free Will.* "The facts tell us," Harris announces like some latter-day Gradgrind,[7] "that free will is an illusion."[8] And it is one we would be better rid of, since in Harris's view it corrupts our moral thinking.

There's a false dilemma here. True, the idea of picking through the various religious options, testing each as if you were evaluating the ripeness of an avocado in the supermarket, is an appealing myth, but nothing more. We'd love to think of ourselves as standing independently over all the possible choices and selecting one (or none) with a dispassionate logic and complete freedom.

But the reality is of course that we don't do anything of the kind. We are a bundle of predispositions and preferences, marked by our experiences and relationships and shaped by our genetic makeup. When we choose, we make a decision *in media res,* in the middle of things, with time ticking away and with events swirling all around us. What's more, contemporary neuroscience is showing how our subconscious is more involved in our decision making than we imagine: it's possible that our making of choices occurs even before we are conscious of making a choice. And yet, even if we can't give a clear philosophical account of why the things we choose to do are real choices, we still have the felt experience of evaluating options and making decisions. It's a felt experience of decision-making for which

7. As that storehouse of facts, Wikipedia, puts it: "Mr Thomas Gradgrind is the notorious headmaster in Dickens's novel *Hard Times* who is dedicated to the pursuit of profitable enterprise. His name is now used generically to refer to someone who is hard and only concerned with cold facts and numbers."

8. Harris, *Free Will,* 5.

we feel (mostly) responsible—except in extreme circumstances, when someone's drug addiction or abusive relationship with his or her father has distorted the choosing. In these cases, it is up to individuals to explain how their experience of decision was inhibited or distorted.

Which means: human beings are capable of evaluating their own decision-making processes—of engaging in self-reflection to the degree that people can give an account for their preferences and biases, and perhaps revising them. While our imagined ability to survey all our options from a neutral standpoint is false, to us is given the ability to reflect on ourselves as choosers and knowers. The gift of human self-consciousness bestows on us this perspective at least; and to that we should add that, as social and historical beings, we have the benefit of others to help us.

Of course, the decision for a particular faith or against it is felt by twenty-first century people to be a highly personal one—as personal as one's sexual preferences or taste in music. That is also a by-product of the Reformation period—the after-effect of a change in theological outlook. That's not to say that the choice is *simply* a matter of personal preference, but that it is felt by many people to be a very private and internal matter. The old cliché about not mentioning religion, sex, and politics in polite company is very much a reality of modern manners—especially regarding religion. To raise the matter is felt to be something of a violation of the other person's personal integrity. Even sex is talked about in public with less reticence. It is also very much the case that the specter of violent religious disagreement hangs over our culture. If we are to live at peace with one another, then it might be better if religion were held to be a purely private matter and not for public discussion.

But I think—and I hope that I can convince you on this score—that we are greatly impoverished by this secretive and private attitude to matters of faith. While it protects us to a degree, it renders us inarticulate about some of the most profound experiences that are given to human beings. We are not challenged to think more deeply about the biggest questions of our lives because we prefer not to discuss them from fear of (perhaps violent) disagreement. We are crippled by this social convention. Personal need not mean entirely private. What I hope for this book is that it will act as an "other" for its reader, sharpening your understanding of what it is you have decided to believe, and why you have decided it.

III **DOES IT WORK?**

We have seen how faith has become, to the contemporary mindset, an option to choose, but at the same time a deeply personal thing that I am not simply free to choose. Another condition that affects what we say we know and believe is the prevailing impact of the philosophy of utilitarianism[9] on Western culture. That is, the criterion for evaluating whether a proposition is to be believed or not is not actually whether it is *true* but whether it *works*. Perhaps I have put the contrast too strongly: it would be hard to imagine that some element of "truth" is irrelevant in most people's thinking about what they believe. Pragmatism is a very powerful consideration, and increasingly so since we think we can measure what works in a public and objective way and thus have an actual discussion about it with others.

This may seem surprising since we live in the age where our heroes and saints are scientists, who seem to have a grasp on tangible reality more than the rest of us and so can pronounce about the truth of the material world with authority. The enduringly popular BBC TV series *Dr Who*, for example, has as its hero a figure who wields scientific knowledge (which in reality is mostly scientific mumbo-jumbo) like a weapon. But the real power of the scientific paradigm is that it appears to work so successfully in making our lives more convenient and pleasurable. It makes truth *work*. "The Truth" itself is, in any case, some distance off from the ordinary person, who cannot possibly hope to evaluate the claims and counter-claims of specialists.

Now, at the same time, many Westerners have found this materialist pragmatism crass and disheartening—and unspiritual. Counting the bottom line is objective, but it isn't pretty. Where's the romance in a spreadsheet? And at that level, it doesn't "work" as it claims it should. It certainly doesn't produce the kind of happy lives that it promises. And so, many Western people have found themselves attracted to Eastern religions and philosophies. The irony is that Westerners cannot even at this point rid themselves of their utilitarianism—because they find that Eastern religion "works" for them. Adopting an Eastern religion isn't for Westerners usually a matter of believing various metaphysical propositions, but rather of experiencing the benefits of religious practices: a better work-life balance,

---

9. Utilitarianism is usually associated with the Victorian-era thinkers Jeremy Bentham and John Stuart Mill. The underlying principle of utilitarianism is usually summarized by the slogan "the greatest happiness of the greatest number."

a more peaceful inner world, opportunities for doing good works and a healthier lifestyle.

What matters for people is what will work in the living of life. And there is certainly a case to be made that the Christian life actually works. Scott Adams of *Dilbert* fame is one who proclaims himself deeply impressed by the *utility* of religion, as we saw above. Strangely, it seems to work.

In a sense the attraction of questions of utility is indisputable: who doesn't want a life that actually works? What I think needs challenging is the criteria by which we think we rightly evaluate whether things are "working" for us. What are these criteria? How can we accurately measure whether they are working or not? Over what period of time should we consider whether something is working? Even to speak of something "working" or not is to admit to some idea of a good—some transcendent measure by which there can be an evaluation.

There are two important things that traditional religious beliefs introduce into the discussion here which make an evaluation by the simple criteria of "does it work" even more complex. The first of these is that human suffering might be redemptive in some way. That is, something that might appear not to be "working" might, through divine intervention or whatever means, turn out to be the epitome of human action. This is an alarming thought for relatively comfortable, pain-free Westerners to confront. And I'd hasten to add that the religions have very different ways of accounting for suffering. Some in the Eastern traditions see suffering as a result of negative karma. Christianity, for its part, names suffering as evil in and of itself, but capable of being woven into the divine plan for extraordinary good.

The second element of most traditional religious belief is that of the afterlife. Again, the religions differ massively on the details of the afterlife: there's heaven, Nirvana, and Valhalla, and they aren't at all the same. But an afterlife of any kind offers a point of evaluation for human life that lies beyond this world. It speaks of a perspective on human life that is beyond our knowing at this point. It relativizes our contemporary evaluations of the viability of the lives we are leading. We cannot yet see what it means for life to "work"; and so we need a framework that gives us more than pragmatic answers to our most profound questions. This may be something even a committed materialist might acknowledge: that it is only at the end of an earthly life that the true evaluation of its effectiveness or its goodness can be contemplated.

IV I WANT TO BELIEVE

There is a kind of wistfulness expressed at this state of affairs, too. With the rise of a dogmatic "New" Atheism, it would be easy to overlook the fact that a kind of longing for the "ability" to believe is widespread. People are taking a pensive look over the back fence of religion. Despite the efforts of the atheist firebrand Christopher Hitchens (1949–2011), people frequently express admiration for aspects of the religious worldview, and for the beneficial effects that religious belief brings to those who are so fortunate. Those who have moved on from a religious past will often express feelings of grief and loss—even when the circumstances of their leaving are quite bitter.

This longing for a religious faith expresses itself in a number of ways. It may exist alongside quite strident criticisms of church behavior. It is found when people describe themselves as "spiritual, but not religious" without ever quite knowing what that is. It appears in the massive subscription of parents to religious schooling for their children.[10] It peeks out when intellectuals speak somewhat wistfully about the impact of the King James Bible or enviously about the beauty of the liturgy and the pleasant security of a habit of churchgoing. It is apparent in the inability of contemporary secular people to match their often powerful moral intuitions to a coherent description of what the moral life might look like for all people.

Well-known Melbourne atheist Dick Gross (1954–) expresses his deep admiration for choral evensong and for the role that religions play in being a "carrier of culture."[11] Alain de Botton's book *Religion for Atheists* is an appreciative (if gratingly twee) account of what survives in and around religion and especially Christianity, and an appeal to non-believers to, in a sense, place their faith in the best of humanity by building temples to the human spirit.[12] British broadcaster Melvyn Bragg (1939–), who published a book about the King James Bible in 2011, argued strongly against the dogmatism of Richard Dawkins (1941–) without ever conceding that he has a faith himself:

> I do believe there are things I can't know. I do believe that there are things beyond the human mind, and oddly enough, I respect

---

10. This is true at least in the UK and in Australia.
11. Gross, "Apostates for Evensong."
12. de Botton, *Religion for Atheists.*

those things and to cadge a lift on faith, for atheists, seems to me a bit of a last resort.[13]

On the other hand, for those who do embrace belief in God believing is not simply a default position. Those who believe are less likely to be the nominal believers of even a few decades ago and are much more likely to hold on to their beliefs as a matter of thought-out conviction. The cost of coming to belief, especially for those who were not born into a certain set of beliefs, is high. Those who do come to faith under those conditions are likely to be more certain about their beliefs, not less. This aspect of contemporary religious sociology perhaps makes religious belief more difficult for those who are less certain—since the standard for faith is set at such a confident measure. But is there a way of believing that is open to the rest of us?

V IS BELIEVING EVEN POSSIBLE ANYMORE?

The purpose of this book is to address the question "what does it mean to believe today?" I think this is an unexamined question for a lot of people, believers and unbelievers alike. We have become unfamiliar with the vocabulary of believing and lost the ability to articulate what it is like to have faith. And yet, there is an enormous hankering after the believing life—a recognition that believing has its benefits. My hope is that this book will alert its readers to the way in which their thoughts about "faith" have been framed in the cultural context of the post-Christendom West.

A couple of powerful suspicions have driven me in my inquiry. One of these, learnt from the English theologian John Milbank (1952–) and the Canadian philosopher Charles Taylor (1931–) in the main, is that theological thinking is everywhere. We can't stop thinking about God, or god-substitutes. Secular culture has talked itself into imagining that a space has been cleared away in which there is no theology at all. This space is strictly policed so that the traditionally religious cannot enter it unless they leave their religious patterns of thought in the cloakroom. In actuality, theological thinking permeates all human interactions. What I mean by "theological thinking" is not just the language of traditional Christian theology, of course. "Theology" names the way in which appeals to transcendent concepts and the reverence shown towards these concepts appear in the

13. Bragg quoted in Ward, "Melvyn Bragg Attacks Richard Dawkins' 'Atheist Fundamentalism.'"

absence of other deities. For example, the Australian journalist and popular historian Peter Fitzsimons (1961–) is well known for his strident atheism. However, he has constructed in its place a national myth of Australian-ness revolving around heroic military virtues, especially as they are expressed in the sporting arena. Fitzsimons's pious devotion to this myth has all the hallmarks of a religion, with himself as its leading theologian.

The pervasiveness of theological thinking means that we are more used to having "faith" than we perhaps think we are. Faith is more commonplace, more normally human, than is often assumed. People do not characteristically ask "what do I have faith in?" but "do I have faith at all?" This is, I think, a subtle but crucial mistake—and one that makes religious belief more awkward, not less. It is a result of our contemporary "turn to the subject," part of our fascination with ourselves rather than that which lies beyond us. Like love, faith has become a subject in itself—seen as a virtue or a condition or a quality of experience worthy of analysis regardless of its object. As a result, the possible objects of faith have become obscured in contemporary discussions.

This ought to matter more than it does. It seems obvious that we could discuss "love" as a feeling in isolation, but that what really matters is the kind of thing or person that attracts one's love. Devotion to Adolf Hitler and devotion to the sport of saber fencing are both forms of devotion; but it is actually not that profound an observation. It is far more intriguing to focus on the differences between the two, and to notice that different objects of devotion make for very different experiences of devoted feelings.

In trying to describe the contemporary culture's approach to religious faith I have developed the habit of asking "what *other* belief systems have emerged when and where traditional Christian theology has faded somewhat from view?" It then remains for us to ask: are these alternatives viable? How do they work? Are they good and beautiful and true? It is worth posing these questions about the quality of the potential objects of our faith, because the focus on whether I (as a *subject*) have any faith at all has made the issue a discussion of whether I have a certain experience, regardless of what I have faith *in*.

The second suspicion is that, though questions of faith and unbelief are often cast in purely rational terms, as if faith is a purely mental exercise of assenting to various truths (or not), the reality is that faith is a matter of the whole human person. A proper description of faith must not avoid the rational, but it cannot avoid the moral, personal, and existential dimensions if it is to be plausible. It has long been noted that human beings do not simply believe the most convincingly rational of arguments. In fact, we would suspect a purely rational human being of being a machine in disguise. This doesn't mean that the business of reasoning about matters of faith is futile, but rather that human beings ought to reflect on their hearts as well as their minds in giving consideration to their patterns of belief. We are likely to believe that which it suits us to believe rather than that which is most true. As the French philosopher Blaise Pascal (1623–62) famously said, "[t]he heart has its reasons of which the reason knows nothing."[14]

Ultimately, that is an indication as to the concern of this book. When we understand something of how we human beings come to know things— to believe them—we will see that the heart and the head are not easily separable. Human beings are, as Augustine of Hippo (354–430) pointed out long ago, desiring creatures. We are essentially looking to (and for) love. The question of what it means to believe in God in the twenty-first century is not simply a matter of mental calculations but involves our deepest longings. That does not mean that the intellect explains nothing; only that it doesn't explain everything.

We begin our exploration by way of Alfred Tennyson (1809–92), the great nineteenth-century poet—the voice in many ways of an age of doubting but at the same time an age of the longing to believe. Next, we perhaps take a strange turn and introduce the Devil, along with the German Reformer Martin Luther (1483–1546). That chapter suggests that our beliefs about God do relate to our sense of ourselves as moral beings. Following this, chapter 4 takes the question of our existence within time and argues that hope and patience are both components of the kind of faith that Christians have always described. The context of making judgments, even personal ones, in the context of "expert knowledge" is taken up in chapter 5. How can we speak of certainty when we are in the hands of specialist knowledge at every turn? Lastly, I put forward the suggestion that Christian faith is a kind of "getting it," not dissimilar to the way we might get a joke. And this is because Christianity itself declares an impossible possibility: it makes a surprising, rather than perhaps obvious, sense.

My own perspective is that of a life-long believer and church attender who has now become a professional theologian. Ordinarily, such qualifications would not lend an air of authenticity to a consideration of believing and not-believing. One of the many cultural myths about religious belief

---

14. Pascal, *Pensées*, 164.

that one hears repeated is that the doubter, or even the ex-believer, is more authentic and more real than the believer; that unbelieving is more courageous than faith. That may in some circumstances be the case, but I don't see that it is universally so. Believing may in many instances cost the believer a great deal, and take immense personal courage.

For my part, I am happy in my faith, though I am aware how blessed I am in living in the time and place that I do. I am not threatened with persecutions, nor am I exposed to ridicule for my faith—well not much. I have not been exposed as yet to a terrible grief that might stretch my faith to the limit. It has brought me a vocation in which I take great pleasure, and I have a comfortable lifestyle. I'd hasten to add—and I feel I need to do so partly because of the cultural myth about belief that I mentioned above—that I do experience intellectual and experiential doubts periodically. Also, as an academic and teacher, I believe I am called to pursue my reasons for believing with as much rigor as I can muster, and that means asking difficult questions of myself and pursuing lines of thought that are uncomfortable.

In offering this piece of autobiographical detail I am aware that it may not buy me any credibility one way or the other with my readers. That is not why I feel it is necessary to "come clean," however. I do so because I am, I hope, aware of my own "context of believing," just as I hope that what is in the following pages will help its readers in considering the cast of their own beliefs—or lack of them.

On the other hand, I am not ashamed of being an orthodox Christian believer who believes in a pretty much orthodox way. There is a kind of book that you'll find sitting on the shelves of secular bookstores under the "religion" section which is a defense of "faith" in abstraction from any but the vaguest object. The word "journey" will no doubt appear somewhere in the title or subtitle of the book. In an effort to be as appealing to potential readers as possible, they make it obvious how much they have moved away from orthodox Christian faith and from the church. This genre has been going around for more than sixty years, and pretty much nothing new is being said today that wasn't said in the 1960s by writers like the English bishop J. A. T. Robinson (1919–83) in his famous book *Honest to God*. The authors—and publishers—seem happily oblivious to the hackneyed nature of this depiction of what it is to believe. Crucially, "faith" becomes not something one has in something transcendent, a divinity or a higher power, but something one simply *has*. Such accounts of faith are appealing because they are individual and thus already seem more authentic. In the end, this is simply narcissistic. They just tell us what they think we want to hear, pretty much.

Like the journalist and novelist G. K. Chesterton (1874–1936) in his book *Orthodoxy*, I would like to show that belief in an orthodox form of Christianity need not be conformist and inauthentic in the slightest. In fact, it is a great and even daring adventure. It asks us to believe in things that are not simply symbols. Even though I take the business of believing and its obstacles as seriously as I can, I am not interested in accounts of religious faith that water everything down in an attempt to look more normal. To put it bluntly: at the center of Christianity is a highly unlikely, nay *impossible,* event: the resurrection from the dead of Jesus of Nazareth. It seems to me that if we can't come at that, then Christian faith has no life at all.

Two

Love, Loss, and Death

There lives more faith in honest doubt, believe me, than in half the creeds.

ALFRED TENNYSON

I THE FAITH AND DOUBT OF ALFRED TENNYSON

The story of the great poet Alfred Tennyson shows how faith and doubt are interwoven with all the other complex business of a life's narrative—our loves, our griefs, and our feelings about death. His sincere and lifelong wrestle with religious belief was part of his equally lifelong struggle to understand himself. As we shall see, this life of this unusual person forms somewhat of a template for the struggle to believe in the post-Enlightenment world that we still very much inhabit.

The son of a gloomy Lincolnshire clergyman, Tennyson arrived at Cambridge University in 1827 already an accomplished and precocious poet. He was a striking young man, standing over six feet tall and with a powerful physique. The mass of his somewhat unkempt black hair was set upon a noble head. His tanned face carried an intense expression of melancholy.

The Somersby rectory had been a dysfunctional household to say the least, with the eleven children largely left to amuse themselves by wandering around the local marshes and fens. If Tennyson was shy at first, his prodigious ability and intensity of personality soon attracted others; and he found some companionship in the secret intellectual club known as "the Apostles," which he was invited to join in 1829. From this convivial if exclusive group came many of Tennyson's most longstanding friendships—including Richard Monckton Milnes, John Sterling, Frederick Maurice (later famous as a theologian), and Richard Trench. He became known by the society as the "Poet of the Apostles."

In Tennyson's second year at Cambridge, another young man arrived at the university who would become the kind of intimate friend that his childhood had lacked. His name was Arthur Hallam, the son of a leading historian and scholar, and in his own way remarkably gifted. Hallam also was invited to join the Apostles.

It is hard to miss just how profound the intimacy of their friendship became. Indeed, Hallam became engaged to Tennyson's sister Emily. They shared not in an amorous passion—that is the fascination of our age—but in the delights of intellectual discovery and in the vigorous discussion of any topic that came to mind. They shared with one another their difficulty they found at maintaining religious belief and yet the sense of loss they felt in not believing. Criticism of the text of the Bible and scientific discoveries about the age of the earth had appeared to challenge the faith of many of the best minds at Cambridge; and Tennyson and Hallam were no different. Certainly, nothing in Tennyson's upbringing at the rectory would have commended orthodox Christian faith to him as anything but a burden to be borne. It held no obvious attraction.

The summer of 1833 began with Hallam spending time at the Tennyson home in rural Lincolnshire, in the English midlands. These were memorable weeks—a sweet time that Tennyson would always remember with some sense of pain because they were never to be repeated. In August, Hallam's father took him on a journey to the European continent. On September 15th, Henry Hallam returned to his hotel in Vienna only to discover Arthur in an armchair, dead of a cerebral hemorrhage.

The blow this struck to Tennyson was overwhelming. His grandson, Sir Charles Tennyson, would later write:

> The sudden extinction of his friend, with all his infinite capacity
> for affection and his brilliant promise, struck at the very roots of

his will to live. Could it really be that all this great spiritual treasure was annihilated: that all human love and all man's spiritual
effort are but a momentary ripple on the ocean of eternity? Was
the world wholly without purpose and man an irresponsible toy
for the gigantic forces of Nature? If so, what value could there be
in life?[1]

If you have ever had a chance to walk about a Victorian graveyard you will
be struck by the openness and even sentimentality with which Victorians
regarded death. To gaze at the headstones in the graveyard of St. Stephen's,
Newtown, near where I live, is to catch a glimpse of tales of real pity. An
infant, her sister, her brother, and her mother follow each other in rapid
succession into the ground. A young man who journeys across the world
on the trail of who knows what dream drowns in Sydney Harbour. We are
not unlike them in that terrible griefs affect us too. But we have less experience of them, and fewer words with which to express our loss. We are
not articulate in the public elaboration of our feelings. We do not feel that
anyone would be interested in our thoughts about the brevity of life and the
nearness of our mortality.

But Tennyson was to make an art form of grieving. He was too sor-
rowed to attend the funeral, and did not visit Hallam's tomb until after he
was married. But he could not stop his poetic muse:

Tears, idle tears, I know not what they mean,
Tears from the depth of some divine despair
Rise in the heart and gather to the eyes,
In looking on the happy Autumn-fields,
And thinking of the days that are no more.

Dear as remembered kisses after death,
And sweet as those by hapless fancy feigned
On lips that are for others; deep as love,
Deep as first love, and wild with all regret;
Death in Life, the days that are no more.

The poem that made Tennyson's career as a poet, "In Memoriam A.H.H.,"
is a lengthy reflection on the death of his friend which did not appear for
seventeen further years. It is a poem of grief at the loss of a dear friend. But
it is also a poem about the pain of losing faith. Tennyson was one of the
great doubters of his age. His was still very much a Christianized society;
and, in general, traditionally orthodox Christian views held sway. Arguably

1. Tennyson, *Alfred Tennyson*, 145.

the mid-nineteenth century was the high watermark of the Christian-
ization of Britain. But as we have noted already: there were a number of
developments in the world of scholarship that seemed to put orthodox
Christianity under some difficulty. Advances in astronomy and geology
seemed to contradict biblical cosmology, at least as it had been traditionally understood. The world was not new, but rather very, very ancient. The
universe was far more vast than had been previously imagined. It seemed
less and less that humankind occupied anything like a significant place in
that universe. If humankind felt small, and lonely, there was at the same
time optimism about human technological progress. This was the age of
the industrial revolution, of the steam engine and the factory. People still
wanted to believe, but wanted to do so in all sincerity given what they now
knew about the world. Was there a way forward for them?

Added to this for Tennyson was the personal existential crisis occa-
sioned by the loss of his friend. It seemed to be exactly the kind of random
occurrence that would characterize a heartless universe. And yet, he was
not ready to give up on faith entirely. Here's a passage from "In Memoriam":

> I falter where I firmly trod,
> And falling with my weight of cares
> Upon the great world's altar-stairs
> That slope thro' darkness up to God,
>
> I stretch lame hands of faith, and grope,
> And gather dust and chaff, and call
> To what I feel is Lord of all,
> And faintly trust the larger hope.

All that is happening and all that has happened to him has led to uncertainty. His feet now "falter," where once before he had been confident of
his footfall upon the ground of faith. His "weight of cares"—primarily his
deep sense of loss for his friend—causes him to fall upon the "world's altar-
stairs." The picture reminds me of the burden the protagonist Christian
carries in John Bunyan's (1628–89) great seventeenth-century Christian
classic *Pilgrim's Progress*. Only this burden is not the poet's sin which is
ultimately to be removed as he approaches the Celestial City, but rather his
"weight of cares" from which there is no evident relief. The path to God (a
stairway to heaven?) is shrouded in darkness. He is not yet ready to declare,
as New York band Talking Heads sang in the 1980s, that this was a "road to
nowhere." But all he can do is reach out his "lame hands of faith, and grope."
He can have no certainty about what he is reaching for, but only in the end

a faint trust. The hands that stretch out are "lame," and can only grope. They are ready to cling if only whatever is on the other side will provide something to cling to.

In the end, the poet grasps at handfuls of "dust and chaff." The "dust and chaff" that he gathers suggests the dust to which Adam is told he will return in Genesis 3 on account of the curse. It is a mark of mortality and an intimation of death. The poet calls, not to a personal God who reveals himself in the traditional and biblical sense, but rather to "what I feel is Lord of all." Who or what is this dark divinity, shrouded in mystery and unknowability? He hopes for a hand to reach out to meet his groping arm, but with no confidence, however much he wishes it. What is the "larger hope"? He doesn't quite know, other than to say that hope is, perhaps inexplicably, part of his experience too.

Tennyson became famous through this poem because its themes of grief, loss, and doubt resonated deeply with his Victorian contemporaries. The twentieth century poet T. S. Eliot (1888–1965) wrote of "In Memoriam": "It is not religious because of the quality of its faith, but because of the quality of its doubt."[2] It was profound in the honesty with which it faced the most difficult and personal questions of all—to do with love and death. It was this very private and solitary poem that led with an irony not lost on Tennyson himself to his appointment to the very public post of Poet Laureate in 1850.

Tennyson was unshaken in his conviction that his friend had lived on in some form; and he never finally rejected belief in the existence of God. One of his last poems was the famous "Crossing the Bar," an expression of hope at life's end as one crosses over from life in this world to the hoped for immortality:

> Twilight and evening bell,
> And after that the dark!
> And may there be no sadness of farewell,
> When I embark;
>
> For tho' from out our bourne of Time and Place
> The flood may bear me far,
> I hope to see my Pilot face to face
> When I have crossed the bar.

2. Eliot, *Essays Ancient and Modern*, 177.

But despite believing in the immortality of the soul and in his "Pilot," it could never be said that he was an orthodox Christian believer in any sense. That conviction had long been shaken loose from him in his sorrows.

II **LOVE AND LOSS**

Though he may seem distant from us in time, Tennyson's wrestle with faith has a very contemporary feel to it. Like us, he was stunned and exhilarated by the pace of technological change. As is the claim in our day, the power of experimental and observational science to explain the natural world seemed to make God somewhat superfluous. The traditional concept of God was, so it seemed, redundant. The lingering ideas of the Enlightenment, applied to biblical studies and to theology more generally, did much to erode confidence that there was revelation of God to be found in the dogmas and creeds of orthodox Christianity. As we have seen, Tennyson was under the impact of this discussion from the late 1820s on.

But these developments did not, then as now, lead to a decline in religious belief as such. Rather, faith sought out new forms. If religious faith could not be established by reason or evidence, perhaps experience might provide an alternative channel to the divine. At the beginning of the nineteenth century, Christian theologians like Friedrich Schleiermacher (1768–1834) began to emphasize the more mystical and experiential aspects of Christian faith. Religious dogmas were not to be taken as direct descriptions of realities but rather as metaphors for encounters with the divine. Though people like Tennyson did not feel that they could any longer accept Christian orthodoxy, they were reluctant to pursue pure atheism. There was inside them a deep conviction that there was something transcendent. Not that they could name it, or give it a face—they could only grope towards it in the dark.

And then there was the experience of love and loss. Perhaps the Victorians in their time, before the wide acceptance and application of Darwinian views, were more ready to sanctify these powerful feelings. Feelings seemed to come from some extra-phenomenal source; to be an intimation of immortality. We naturalize things. We are now more ready to see the pains and joys of human fellowship as demanded of us by our biological selves than as evidence of a holiness that is beyond us. As we saw in the first chapter, the popular sense of the "spiritual" remains in many people, and permeates these moments at which heart is most evidently exposed. It is in our most intimate relationships that we feel most connected to the truth about who we are as individuals and most certain about our steps into the world; and we have the gratifying experience of being able to provide this for others.

Death remained, and remains, the final, impermeable barrier. Poets of the sixteenth and seventeenth centuries like John Donne (1572–1631) certainly feared death as the curtailment of love and the rotting of the human body. Death was a demonic, personified figure who stalked his victims. Donne needs to draw on all the resources of his Christian faith to repudiate it in "Death Be Not proud." But the lament of the nineteenth century wails in a different key—one that we moderns more readily recognize as our own. The loss is not felt as the result of being tyrannized by a sinister force. It is now a brute fact in a remorseless universe that is governed only by a God who remains unmoved at the plight of the creatures who experience it. To face death or to grieve is not be part of a dramatic struggle in which the darkness of Mordor has temporarily got the upper hand. It is at least possible to express rage against that force. Death for a Tennyson and for we his twenty-first-century descendants is sad and bewildering. It flaps its wings in the face of our confidence in human technological mastery of the world. It too is a darkness—but not the darkness of a Mordor. It is a darkness of not knowing.

III FEELING IT

What we have in the life of Alfred Tennyson is the story of a person who is caught in the bind between belief and unbelief. Like many twenty-first-century people, he was not ready to concede everything to mere materialism; but he was certainly not compelled by anything like an orthodox Christian faith.

It may be the case that a terrible and sudden experience of grief becomes the trigger for persons to doubt their faith in a way they have not done until that point. The seeds of Tennyson's powerful grief were sown in the years well before Hallam's death. Tennyson was already a doubter and had already sought solace in mysticism. Powerful and shocking though it was, the loss of his friend was interpreted through the lens of his already quavering religious belief and not the other way around. Certainly, his faltering was magnified by his anguish; but it was not caused by it. It is a point worth making because the way we interpret an experience is often determined by beliefs we already have in place. Tennyson's grief became the megaphone for his doubt, but in theory he could have written much of "In Memoriam" without it.

As we can see with Alfred Tennyson, doubt can have a peculiar relationship with conviction. The shape of his lifelong reaching after the divine was set in train by his prior decision to accept the premises of the philosophical and critical thinking of his day. The great German philosopher Immanuel Kant (1724-1804) had divided reality into two realms—the "phenomena," or the material, everyday world accessible by our senses, and the "noumena," or that part of reality, including perhaps God, to which we have no access by our senses. Kant was no atheist, but he insisted that we have to deal in the phenomenal world and not in the noumena. Religious faith must therefore take a highly individualistic and mystical form.

This is fine for those who have religious experiences that they can point to as a means to authenticate their faith. There are of course many of those. The American psychologist and philosopher William James (1842–1910) made an extensive inventory of religious experiences at the turn of the nineteenth century and recounted and classified them in his classic work *The Varieties of Religious Experience*. James wrote:

> When we survey the whole field of religion, we find a great variety in the thoughts that have prevailed there; but the feelings on the one hand and the conduct on the other are almost always the same, for Stoic, Christian, and Buddhist saints are practically indistinguishable in their lives.[3]

James was not about to build a proof for the existence of God in the traditional sense on the basis of the filing cabinet full of testimony to religious experiences that he had collected and collated. He was confident to conclude that this wealth of data exposed something anthropological, in the sense that "the conscious person is continuous with a wider self through which saving experiences come."[4] That is to say, there is always more to the self than the self is aware of; and this subconscious self is evidence that there is more life in us than we even know ourselves. For James as for Tennyson, these outer limits of the personality point to a "mystical" or even "supernatural" dimension in which the human being shares—a dimension that is no less real in being unseen, because it produces real effects.

---

3. James, *The Varieties of Religious Experience*, 366.

4. Ibid., 373.

Experience appears to offer a rationally incontrovertible gateway to the transcendent realm. I may not be able to believe that certain events happened in history or that certain propositions are true as they are stated—though they may be true in some symbolic way perhaps—but I do know my own experience. There is an authenticity to the beatings of my own heart that I cannot deny. It is subjective and personal and thus not on the table of public reason. It seems to be parked safely in the cul-de-sac of the heart and off the troublesome highways of philosophical criticism. As James wrote, "Feeling is private and dumb, and unable to give an account of itself."[5] Experience, it is often forgotten, requires interpretation and articulation to become something meaningful. But even so: *it is real.*

Or so it seems. There are those who testify that they do not have that religious sense. There are also those who are skeptical of religious experience as merely a function of the human brain, a by-product of our evolution that conveys (somehow) an advantage to religious people (and religious communities) in the bloody business of natural selection. In the stark and rather bitter words of Radiohead: "just 'cos you feel it, doesn't mean it's there." The certainty that an inner spiritual illumination appears to offer is not, in fact, so certain. That's not to say that being able to observe the neurological patterns of the believing brain can disprove religious or mystical experience, only that it takes away that sense that feeling it makes it inconvertibly true—however much it feels like it. Experience is not the complete dead end that skeptics would like it to be, as William James's extraordinary compilation of testimony must surely show. But experience alone is not enough.

IV A MORE UNCERTAIN UNCERTAINTY?

We don't form our beliefs—or our doubts—in isolation from each other. It is likely that if one belief fades in our constellation of beliefs, another will begin to shine more brightly. It is also the case that though we like to think of the process of thought as growing naturally up from certain well established fundamental beliefs, we do not actually form our beliefs in such a linear and orderly fashion. Believing is not a laboratory exercise. Doubt will not grow in isolation, but it is the counterpart to a growing faith elsewhere. As philosopher Ludwig Wittgenstein (1889–1951) once said:

5. Ibid., 315.

> If you tried to doubt everything you would not get as far as doubting anything. The game of doubting itself presupposes certainty.[6]

If we are to be honest, the things we believe with most certainty are not merely those propositions which are, by dint of logic alone, most demonstrable. The truest of truths are those that somehow captivate us. Those are the truths that can awaken in us the longings of our hearts. Religious dogmas can lie flat on the dusty page, unenlivened by any spirit. They can be rehearsed and recited, but remain unreal. They can seem almost stupefying in their abstraction from anything that matters. That has been the experience of many people, especially those who (like Tennyson) have grown up in the Christian faith.

By contrast, the power of what we might call "Enlightenment humanism"—that view of the world in which human reason reigns supreme as an instrument for analyzing and interpreting what we see—is not just that it claims that it *explains* the world, but that it also promises us that we will be able to *master* that world. It offers us the holy grail of control over our environment. With control comes security, and with security, the opportunity for pleasure. What could be simpler?

The Enlightenment worldview can actually help us to do the things we want to do. That sounds rather banal when I write it like that; but the promise makes our hearts leap for joy. It is an invitation to taste of the gleaming fruit of the tree of rationalism—technology. Empirical science does not impress us merely by its theories and explanations. It succeeds inasmuch as it unleashes the power of the machine. Its shout of triumph is the roar of the dual engine of the Bugatti Veyron, with 16 cylinders and nearly 1000 brake horsepower. Its glory is the shiny gleam of the nose of the bullet train scudding across Japan, and the illumination of all the cities of the globe visible from the Airbus 330. In those cities there seems to be no day and night. It entrances with the way in which it turns imagination into possibility and brings fantasy into fruition. Science fiction becomes reality in our lifetimes.

Technological change is an exhilarating ride to be on. And what's not to like? Far too often, people, and often religious people, pretend than they can ignore or write off the astonishing success that humankind has had with technological progress in the last two centuries. We tap away at our laptops, fly around the globe and expect the oncologist to treat our cancer,

6. Wittgenstein, *On Certainty*, §115.

but still manage to sneer at the accomplishments of the worldview that enabled us to produce all of these things.

Whatever our nostalgia for the past, almost no one wants to return to it.

But at the same time, faith in technological progress shows all the hallmarks of religion. For one thing, it tells a story. It narrates the progress of humankind from a dimly remembered but grimy past to an unforeseeable and glorious horizon. Occasionally, a prophet of this sect will pop up with a declaration that nirvana has been attained. But more often the story is told assuming we are in the middle of the journey, with the Promised Land lying ahead. If only we will acquiesce to our technological present, we will have opened before us an extraordinary vista of bodily enhancement, labor-saving devices, and home entertainments. It's a narrative in which a kind of freedom is on offer. Through our machines, we are better able to deflect chance and bad luck, and live the lives we want as opposed to the lives we have been given.

In Kevin Kelly's (1952–) book *What Technology Wants,* he argues that what he calls the "technium" is not simply an inert pile of tools waiting in a toolshed for us to use them, but has actually developed a consciousness (well, almost) of its own:

> . . . after 10,000 years of slow evolution and 200 years of incredible intricate exfoliation, the technium is maturing into its own thing. Its sustaining network of self-reinforcing processes and parts have given it a noticeable measure of autonomy.[7]

By "technium" Kelly means the whole system of technologies operating in concert (as opposed to specific instances of technology, like the iPhone or the food processor). And this system has, as he reads it, the properties of personal agency. It is not too far-fetched to say that the technium

> wants what we want—the same long list of merits we crave. When a technology has found its ideal role in the world, it becomes an active agent in increasing the options, choices, and possibilities of others.[8]

We would not be so crass as to worship a single tool—to bow down before the edge-trimmer or the color printer. But the *technium!* Now that's a different matter altogether. It has something of the aura of divinity about it. Even

7. Kelly, *What Technology Wants,* 12–13.
8. Ibid., 269.

though it is material and simply indicates the transferal of power and information along circuits and optical fibers, it has a glorious metaphysical mystique that has us transfixed in awe, a *mysterium tremendum et fascinans*.[9]

It is worth asking: is our faith well placed? Is there room for doubt *here*? As I have said already, we cannot with any credibility deny our debt to the machines. But isn't it interesting that the dreamers and visionaries among us can rarely contemplate a technology-dominated future without expressing grave misgivings? For all their inventiveness, is it not more often the case that the genre of science fiction in film and in literature offers a dystopian vision of the future? For an example we might take Fritz Lang's (1890–1976) extraordinary 1927 silent film *Metropolis*, in which a mechanized society leads to liberty and leisure for the few that live in the skyscraper aptly named "the New Tower of Babel," and to drudgery for those who serve the demonic machines below the surface. Novelists and filmmakers, who usually begin with some technological marvel—androids perhaps, or deep space travel—are, like all storytellers, really interested in the human. And they know how deeply ambivalent our relationship to progress is. Is not *Metropolis* strangely prophetic of the contemporary nexus between the air-conditioned castles of consumption in the West that depend upon the grinding sweatshops of Asia?

This is the where absolute faith in rationalism and progress, however much it delights our hearts, begins to crumble. The problem is not so much with reason or with technology. It is with human beings. Faith in the inexorable march of progress down the "ringing grooves of change" (to use Tennyson's phrase) depends on a blind faith in humanity. It forgets that the profit motive, which prompts most technological progress, is selfish to the core. It is overlooks human recidivism with a sunny belief that our errors are merely mistakes. It imagines that somehow human beings are going to overcome their implacable hatred of one another and cooperate rather than compete. It has amnesia about the way in which a cult of mass death on an industrial scale has accompanied the onward march of reason and technology. Above all, it offers no check to human pride. This was evident to all at the end of the First World War—the optimism about human enlightenment lay mired in the battlefields of France, drowning in mud and

---

9. Literally: "fearful and fascinating mystery." This was the phrase that the German scholar of religion Rudolf Otto coined in his book *The Idea of the Holy* (first published in German in 1917) to describe the awestruck feeling common to religious experience in different faiths.

mustard gas. But the faith persists in this divinity. What it can do for us, we feel, outweighs the sacrifices we make to it.

The tale of human hubris, learnt at the cost of incredible suffering, had already been told, but had been suppressed. The Bible offers a sustained critique of human over-reaching—a critique that peeps through as a cultural memory in films like *Metropolis*. The Tower of Babel from Genesis 11 is one tale that stands as an emblem of human ambition thwarted. But the whole narrative of the people of Israel itself is a salutary lesson in the cost to human beings themselves of their own pride. Scripture's specific diagnosis is that this pride has at its core a rejection of the authority of God. It isn't that our raising of civilizations and ordering of the world is condemned *per se*. It is when we seek in these things to "make a name" for ourselves independent of the creator that things go awry.

Of course, in the nineteenth century the propositions of orthodox Christianity were not in place to make a successful challenge to the new story now being told—a state of affairs that remains today for many people. Part of the project of the new rationalism was to dismember the text of scripture to the point that it seemed unable to sustain the kind of truth claims it allegedly supported. It exercised a great skepticism against Christianity. But more than that: it made a counter-claim against the goodness and beauty of the Christian life. It appeared to tell a superior tale of human existence and to offer a better hope. The life was bled out of orthodox Christianity.

V DEATH AGAIN

It was scarcely a fair comparison, since orthodox Christianity was depicted as lifeless and loveless. The disappearance of the Christian view of the world was a great tragedy because of what people like Tennyson and ourselves would have to face. It would rob them of a way to endorse the great achievements of the age without becoming blind to the dangers of human pride. Death cut across their confidence in the all-encompassing worldview of rationalism. The overwhelming sense of something other remained, but it became un-expressible. The hollow darkness of death is no less terrifying in its way than the thought that death is a personal force. What is evil, after all, if it isn't nothingness?

We can't forget death; for death certainly hasn't forgotten us. And this means for all our faith in the coming technological heaven-on-earth, we

cannot hope to experience it for long. The promise we cling to in technological advancement is really the promise that adheres to all human living:
that it is part of something more, that it is a part of something bigger and
more impressive. God

> has made everything beautiful in its time. He has also set eternity
> in the human heart; yet no one can fathom what God has done
> from beginning to end (Eccl 3:11).

Yet this sense we have, if it has no language with which it might be articu-
lated, remains a source of bewilderment. No matter how hard we tell ourselves that the material is all we see, we cannot help but grieve with longing.

In 1996, the Australian novelist Helen Garner (1942–) wrote about
a trip to the crematorium, where she had held in her hand the ashes of a
dead child:

> . . . on my way home I had, for the first time in my life, a convic-
> tion—I mean not a thought but knowledge—that life can't possibly
> end at death. I had the punctuation wrong. I thought it was a full
> stop, but it's only a comma, or a dash—or better still, a colon: I
> don't believe in heaven or hell, or punishment or reward, or the
> survival of the ego; but what about energy, spirit, soul, imagina-
> tion, love? The force for which we have no word? How preposter-
> ous, to think that it could die![10]

Like Tennyson, Garner could not gainsay her experience with her rationalism. Sloughing off the Bible's story about human life and death leaves her
with this powerful conviction, but nowhere to ground it.

In the subsequent two decades, Garner has found herself returning to
the Bible, and even, to her own surprise, to church. It has changed her writing about death. Her 2008 novel *The Spare Room* tells the story of Nicole, a
woman in her sixties who is dying of cancer, and her friend, named Helen
(obviously the persona of the novelist herself), with whom she comes to
stay while she undergoes a bizarre alternative therapy. Nicole's desperation
to stay alive and her refusal to accept the inevitability of death drives her
host to distraction. Like many who find themselves nursing the dying, she
becomes extremely angry—with the alternative doctors who seem to be
fleecing her gullible friend, and with the patient, Nicole.

Especially galling is when Nicole tells a third friend that "poor Helen"
isn't coping. This leads Helen to muse:

10. Garner, *True Stories*, 229.

Death will not be denied. To try is grandiose. It drives madness
into the soul. It leaches out virtue. It injects poison into friendship,
and makes a mockery of love.[11]

The alternative therapy, to Helen, is clearly bogus. To Nicole it represents a
chance for healing, but she is deluded. It harms Nicole physically, but also
makes her impossible to love. It obscures the real Nicole, and prevents her
from preparing for what all human beings must face. Its falseness distorts
her terribly, as a person.

Religions can be like that, including forms of Christianity. Fantasies of
all kinds can be used to eclipse death, but at the cost of the truth. Because
human knowledge is limited and fallible, even at its best, we are vulnerable,
especially when we are desperate, to the appearance of the wonder cure, or
the theory that answers every question. Indeed, our faith in our rationality
and medical expertise can be held in precisely this way, too.

Helen is battered by what she experiences with Nicole. But she does
turn to her Christian friend, Lucy, with her questions—and asks in the end
for her blessing, which is sensitively given. Lucy says to Helen:

"Sometimes," she said, "there's only one prayer to say. Lamb of
God. You take away the sin of the world."[12]

From Garner's narrative you get the sense that human beings need to be
open to their own weakness, fear, and dependence on others if they are to
be truly themselves. Far from obscuring the reality of our weakness and
vulnerability before death, Helen finds that Christian faith helps to accept
it. Christian faith is not a frankly dishonest denial of the reality of death,
but a hope that in the Lamb of God there is a greater reality on the other
side of our failure.

Lucy's prayer certainly expresses more than Garner's initial conviction that death is not the end. It is not this time a prayer groping into an
unknown abyss. It is addressed specifically to someone known: to the Lamb
of God—the title given to Jesus by John the Baptist. It is not that grief is to
be avoided by this prayer, or denied. But the yearning that comes with it is
directed to a divinity who grieves, and who tastes death.

That is how his story runs. *The story*: this is what was removed from
the Christian faith by the rationalism of the end of the eighteenth century.
It filleted orthodox belief down to a set of bare propositions. It put aside

11. Garner, *The Spare Room*, 89.
12. Ibid., 100.

the very dynamic of the message and instead attempted to look beyond it to something supposedly more real. When this proved undiscoverable or undesirable, the Christian faith itself was discarded in its orthodox form—and sometimes altogether.

Out in the fields, outside of the walls of the university towns and far from the cloisters of the established church, a very different faith was being preached. The faith of the evangelical revivals was as lively and whole as the alternative rejected by Tennyson was flat and dull. In the sermons of John Wesley (1703–91) and George Whitefield (1714–70) was a message to enthrall and to enliven. They told a story that meshed with experience and that inflamed hearts with love for God. It produced an overflow of remarkable deeds that were far more than the mere love of human achievement could have ever accomplished. There was a three-dimensionality to this faith, whatever its more cultured despisers may have thought about it.

❦

In examining the faith and doubts of Alfred Tennyson we have been able to see how the structure of belief is not simply a matter of reasoning alone, but has to do with one's whole self, including one's experiences in the world. We believe some things because we doubt some others. The powerful experiences of death and grief shape our beliefs more than we perhaps even know. Our next task is to take this consideration even more seriously; and to put the individual into the path of a judgement. The prayer to the "Lamb of God" is the prayer that recognises that humanity lives in a sometimes quiet desperation, in need of a Lamb "who takes away the sin of the world." If we are to consider our whole selves as believing or doubting creatures, we must consider what this means for ourselves as moral beings. When we do, we find to that a prosecutor lies ready to spring to his feet.

THREE

The Devil He Does

We are each our own devil, and we make this world our hell.

OSCAR WILDE (1854–1900)

I DOES HE, OR DOESN'T HE?

If the devil exists, he pesters you with doubts. One of his tricks, if he exists, is to get to you to doubt even his existence. In which case, if he doesn't exist, then attack was merely a projection of something in you. He has no power; it is a toothless attack. Ha!

But wait. Weren't you just a minute ago convinced that he, or something like him, was real? Didn't you hear him speaking to you, as sure as eggs? Now you say he doesn't exist! Can you trust yourself, then, to know reality from fantasy? Isn't it *you*, in fact, who is unraveling?

You're on a roll now. Did that dark thought you had never conceived before emerge from the sweaty locker rooms of your own soul? That plausible devil: he's your own creation, then?

So, let's assume he does exist for a moment—a potent and irresistible spiritual force attacking you. What chance have you got to stand against him? If you don't doubt the devil, how can you defeat him?

These are the *wiles of the devil*—or some of 'em.

II THE WRESTLE

If only the experience of wrestling the devil was as dramatic as it sounds in The Epistle to the Ephesians:

> Put on the whole armor of God, so that you may be able to stand against the wiles of the devil. For our struggle is not against enemies of blood and flesh, but against the rulers, against the authorities, against the cosmic powers of this present darkness, against the spiritual forces of evil in the heavenly places. (Eph 6:11–12)

We are to imagine the believer striding out like Luke Skywalker to clash light sabers with the devil. He is easy to spot because he wears black, and rides a Harley, and has some serious tattooing on his right arm detailing how he'll dismember the mothers of those who stand in his way.

But that's not how it goes. The devil—if it *is* him—always comes in disguise. *Even Satan disguises himself as an angel of light.* Or, as something less than an angel of light. He speaks reasonably to reasonable people. He makes a good deal of quiet sense, in a completely perverse way. His talk has, (as Rowan Williams [1950–] puts it) an "Escher-like quality, landscapes turning inwards on themselves in visual but plausible absurdity."[1] It's the kind of remorseless, undefeatable logic that drives you to insanity. It's psychopathic.

Ivan Fyodorovich Karamazov is the most rationalistic and agnostic of the three Karamazov brothers in Dostoyevsky's (1821–81) great novel, *The Brothers Karamazov.* Yet it is he who has a nightmarish encounter with the devil. The devil comes to him in the guise of a rather ingratiating and certainly not very frightening middle-aged man, looking a little down on his luck. He's a "banal devil," a "sponger." Is he a vision, or is he real? Does he have an independent existence, or is he a parasite (a "sponger") on Ivan's fevered imagination? Does he come from within Ivan, or from some source without? Ivan says to him:

> I sometimes don't see you, and don't even hear your voice, as last time, but I always guess what you're driveling because *it is I, I myself who am talking and not you!*[2]

1. Williams, *Dostoevsky*, 40.
2. Dostoevsky, *The Brothers Karamazov*, 637.

So, the challenge is for the devil to produce a thought in Ivan that he has never thought before. He says:

> Though I am your hallucination, even so, as in a nightmare, I say original things, such as have never entered your head before, so that I'm not repeating your thoughts at all, and yet I am merely your nightmare and nothing more.[3]

He is prepared to concede to not existing; for that would be a triumph for him. What kind of creature, if that *is* the right word, becomes more powerful the less convinced we are that he exists?

The battle is dramatized in the Ephesians letter exactly because this clash doesn't look obvious. It is called it a war because it looks like a friendly chat. It is hard to see it for what it is. The nature of this confrontation is that it always makes you wonder whether there actually *is* a confrontation. It whispers to you of your own paranoia.

It isn't that there are two side-by-side realities—a kind of mundane level reality that conceals a more dramatic world within. That kind of crass dualism is only ever evoked in scripture as device by which the two-sidedness of flesh and blood existence is revealed to us. The ordinary world *is* the world of spiritual battles.

You're standing right in it.

III MARTIN LUTHER'S DEVIL

The great German Reformer Martin Luther has been described by one of his many biographers, the Dutchman Heiko Oberman (1930–2001), as "a man between God and the devil."[4] But this description shouldn't be thought of as placing Luther permanently betwixt and between, caught in a lifelong wrestle. There was in Luther's life a turning point. The portraits that we have of Luther tell their own story of his life as a life in which there was a major change. There's the thin Luther, gaunt and wasting away through his severe spiritual disciplines and through worry for his own soul; and there's the fat Luther, the man of beer and sausages, full of bonhomie and swagger.

So what happened? In the 1950s, the psychoanalyst Erik Erikson (1902–94) wrote a biography of Luther called *Young Man Luther*. Placing Luther on his couch, Erikson accounted for the transition in Luther's

---

3. Ibid., 639.
4. Oberman, *Luther*.

character as a resolution of his deep identity crisis. He painted the young monk as a gifted individual in "acute psychic despair." Luther's theology gave him a way of articulating his psychological state:

> . . . Luther's definition of man's condition—while part and parcel of his theology—has striking configurational parallels with the inner dynamic shifts like those which clinicians recognize in the recovery of individuals from psychic distress.[5]

Erikson figured that Luther's *theological* breakthrough had come because he had finally found a resolution to his incessant self-questioning. For Erikson, Luther's relationship with his father, the miner Hans Luther, was the source of his apparently spiritual, but in fact psychological troubles. Projecting his fear of his stern father onto the Father of all, Luther could find nothing to comfort him.

They were troubles of a more visceral nature, too: this was another element that Erikson drew in to his depiction. The older Luther made an off-hand comment about having made his breakthrough while "*in cloaca*"—namely, the toilet. Like many people of his era, Luther was prone to gastrointestinal troubles of one kind or another, and was not shy of talking about them. For Erikson, nothing could be clearer: Luther was moving from an anal retentive to an anal explosive phase of life. The moment of great insight was literally gut-wrenching. His movement from the darkness of doubt to the light of faith was in essence a movement of his bowels.

But Erikson's analysis of Luther suffers from inattention to the actual historical evidence, as many historians have noted since. He relies overly on the older Luther's own anecdotes—often told to amuse (!) his dining companions—about his childhood experiences. He suspends the great bridges of his analysis by the slenderest of historical hairs. Since he cannot accept that Luther's theological thinking has any reality to it, Erikson reduces it to a projection of his inner world. Luther inhabited a world in which one could address God, and in which one had to deal with the torments of the devil. Erikson cannot accept that this world has any reality, and so any theological talk must be a code for some other state of affairs, a way of expressing oneself in particular circumstances. There is no line between superstition and religion, for Erikson; so he feels at liberty to interpret religious talk as being about something else other than what it purports to describe. Erikson reduces the genuinely spiritual and theological aspects

---

5. Erikson, *Young Man Luther*, 206.

of Luther's life to the psychological—as if theology is only a way of talking about psychology.

Though making historical errors is grave, it is the second of the two problems with his work that is the more serious. That a psychological explanation, however tenuous, can be made to explain in full the spiritual or theological language that a person speaks is reductionistic. This reductionism is characteristic of modern thinkers for whom theological language is, by definition, not granted any purchase on the real world. The German philosopher Ludwig Feuerbach (1804–72), for example, argued that all human talk of God was simply a projection of ourselves on a large screen. "God" is simply a way of externalizing our very human and very earthly inner struggles and wishes. Theology is simply anthropology, and no more. God is made in the image of man, not the other way around.

Feuerbach's anthropological view of religion complemented the three great anti-theological movements in the latter part of the nineteenth century and the beginning of the twentieth: Marxism, Darwinism, and Freudianism. These three great materialisms all, in their different ways, take it as axiomatic that religious language must be a cypher for some other longing that lies within the human heart, whether it be sex, or capital, or just surviving and passing on one's genes. Each then provides its own, totalizing explanation for the human condition, without remainder. God is simply surplus to requirements.

Sigmund Freud (1856–1939), for example, saw that religion had provided a means for human beings to find security against the terrible randomness and sheer power of nature. This is a very useful function for religious beliefs to serve; but nevertheless, all religious beliefs are ultimately "illusions and insusceptible of proof."[6] Modern, sophisticated human beings have nothing to fear from the disappearance of religious belief and indeed ought to pursue it. But of course Freud was clearing the ground in order that he might build his own edifice upon it. Psychoanalysis, not religion, was intended to provide the transcendent explanation of human existence, and the solution to all its woes. Freud and his disciples were to be the master interpreters of the data of human life.

Each of the three theories offers itself as *the* key to understanding human drives and as the single most powerful explanation for the shape of human civilization; and yet exists right alongside other, equally powerful, totalizing explanations. Marx (1818–83), Darwin (1809–82), and Freud

6. Freud, *The Future of an Illusion*, 27.

each produced accounts of human behavior that were held (at least by their interpreters) to do God out of a job. The old "problem of evil" was drained of its force entirely since, on each description, human maladjustment had an entirely material, or "natural," explanation. The human individual was presumed innocent and only made guilty by the combination of social, historical, and economic forces working upon him or her.

Each view has had a powerful impact on global civilization, not least because of the completeness of the picture that each offers. But the very presence of *three* systems of thought each claiming to provide a complete description of human existence means that, at the very least, each theory cannot be all there is to say about it. Not that they are mutually exclusive necessarily, not at all. Indeed, there have been many intellectuals who have put forward a kind of blended psychoanalytical and Marxist theory. This shows, however, that each theory leaves room for more to be said about the world than they offer. It is the claim for exclusivity that is the least plausible thing about them. And if it is the case that more than one interpretation of reality might be admitted to have some purchase, then why is there not also room for a religious or metaphysical explanation of things *alongside* them? If the completeness of each grand theory is its chief weapon against God, then each must be counted as failing to exclude the possibility of God.

Erik Erikson's psychoanalytical depiction of Luther is basely reductionistic. Nevertheless, Erikson was right in observing this: that Luther is a fascinating study in the psychology of faith and doubt. Erikson's reductionism is a warning against a form of reductionism that lies on the other side—to imagine Luther as simply a theologian, a man of pure mind and spirit, with no parents, no fears, and no bowels. Luther was a whole man: an academic, but also a man of prayer; a scholar but also a preacher. He ate, drank, and shat. His radical insight was not merely a matter of rational conviction, but also a matter of deep personal spiritual necessity. It is true that Luther did say much later in life, possibly when he was in his cups, that he had come to his great insight about the grace of God while in the *cloaca*. And it was true that Luther had deeply disappointed father Hans when he entered a monastery. This snap decision had come when the young Luther was caught in a severe storm and terrified by a thunderbolt landing beside him. Fearing for his life, he called out to St. Anne to save him. As he walked away damp but alive, he vowed to dedicate his life to the service of God.

We can only speculate as to Luther's frame of mind as he entered the monastery. But we do know that Luther's was not a quiet soul. Luther was the master surveyor of the topography of his conscience. He checked it constantly, but always found bumps and hollows. He could not see anything within but the wreckage of his life. He could not, by his own account, feel that the holiness and purity of the righteous God meant anything but death and destruction to him. What he saw was a self-curved-in-upon-itself, by turns proud and disgusted. Though this frustrated his confessor, Johannes Staupitz, who must have become catatonically bored listening to Luther rehearse his minuscule faults, he determined to talk through the troubles of his conscience with the utmost seriousness. How could a man of sin stand confident in the presence of a truly holy God? He could find no such confidence.

Out of the shady areas strode forth his tormentor.

IV FACING THE ACCUSER

Luther recalled later:

> It is not a unique, unheard-of thing for the Devil to thump about and haunt houses. In our monastery in Wittenberg I heard him distinctly. For when I began to lecture on the Book of Psalms and I was sitting in the refectory after we had sung matins, studying and writing my notes, the Devil came and thudded three times in the storage chamber as if dragging a bushel away. Finally, as it did not want to stop, I collected my books and went to bed. I still regret to this hour that I did not sit him out, to discover what else the Devil wanted to do . . . But when I realized that it was Satan, I rolled over and went back to sleep again.[7]

Here he sounds almost jaunty, blasé, as if there was nothing unusual about the Devil poking around in the dining room. He talks about the Devil as if he was some rat or some other animal making an unwanted noise. Though we hear him talk in this flippant way about his encounters with the Devil, we can also infer what nighttime torments for the Luther in his monkish cell must have been like:

> When I awoke last night, the Devil came and wanted to debate with me; he rebuked and reproached me, arguing that I was a sinner. To this I replied: Tell me something new, Devil! I already know that perfectly well; I have committed many a solid and real sin. Indeed there must be good honest sins—not fabricated and

7. Quoted in Oberman, *Luther*, 105.

invented ones—for God to forgive for His beloved Son's sake, who took all my sins upon Him so that now the sins I have committed are no longer mine but belong to Christ. This wonderful gift of God I am not prepared to deny [in my response to the Devil], but want to acknowledge and confess.[8]

The Devil visited him not to frighten him by simply being a creature from the underworld or some kind of cartoonish monster with horns on his head and a pointed tail. That in the end is laughable. The Devil—or to give him one of his biblical names, *Satan*, literally "the accuser"—has his real power in telling us the truth about ourselves. He is a pin-striped barrister, smoothly prosecuting the case against us, drawing up a record of what we will and what we do, reminding us of our moments of remorse and telling us things about ourselves we had only begun to realise.

For an Erikson or a Freud, the notion of "sin" is as superstitious as the rest of religion. Guilt appears as a symptom of a disease—as a sickness of the psyche in need of the soothing balm of analysis. The impact of this view has been pervasive. As the Canadian philosopher Charles Taylor points out, with this shift in framework "what was formerly sin is often now seen as sickness."[9] The results of this culture-wide shift in thinking have been ambivalent at best. On the one hand, it appears as if it elevates human dignity by describing its problems not in moral or spiritual terms but in therapeutic ones. The response to the human plight is care and cure, not condemnation. Surely that is an uplifting alternative?

But—and this seems counter-intuitive to us perhaps—a great deal is lost if the notion of sin and evil is thought to have been superseded. Being sick is simply something that happens to you as an organism, and of which you are almost always the victim. Even an addict who injects herself repeatedly with a poisonous drug is considered to be in the grip of an illness, and merely pitiable. There is nothing put before the human person that challenges her to take responsibility for her actions or to seek change through great wisdom, or a personal conversion. The much-vaunted freedom that was promised to individuals by the polemic against the ideas of sin, evil, and guilt proves to be an illusion. Telling us that our troubles afflict us because we are actually sick introduces us to a kind of fatalism in which we have to accept that we are incapacitated by our lack of health and should submit to treatment by the growing barrage of experts ready on

8. Quoted in ibid., 105–6.

9. Taylor, *A Secular Age*, 618.

hand with the newest pharmaceutical and therapeutical solutions. Psycho-analysis, like other proposed therapies, proves to be of limited diagnostic value because it explains guilt and remorse and shame away. These are not pointers to something *wrong*, but only to something *ill*. As Taylor says, "evil has the dignity of an option for an apparent good; sickness has not."[10] We know well that a psychopath, who does not feel remorse at all, has a kind of anaesthesia of the soul. Could it be that neuro-normal people have the capacity to feel guilt because there are things to feel guilty about?

That is not to say that there is nothing in psychoanalysis. At the very least it has the virtue of inviting the individual to describe some of the aspects of the inward person. The Christian understanding of the human person as created for the fulfillment of a sublime purpose in the service of the Creator, but distorted through a fall for which all are to blame, does not mean that the problem of sin and evil is purely a spiritual one. On the con-trary; we understand from this account that we are both the perpetrators and the victims of evil; and that the call remains for us to aspire to a better form of life. Freudian accounts of the human psyche may very well trace my aberrant desires or my violent temper to my relationship with my father or to some event in my anal retentive phase that hampered my growth to full mature personhood. They may even thereby gain some purchase on my problems to the extent that they are addressed. But none of this removes the necessity of treating me as a responsible agent, a person who acts and who potentially acts and who ultimately to be able to explain why he did what he did.

Explain? To whom must I explain myself? Ultimately, talk about hu-man morality or "spirituality" must pose this question. It implies a court; a bar of judgement. There must be a standard against which human life is to be judged; and indeed, a judge. If we are "responsible" beings, we must fi-nally be called upon to give an answer. We cannot within ourselves contain the means of our own judgement. Even the invitation to "do what seems best to you" implies the concept of a "best" learnt from somewhere outside of oneself. There must be a reference point, a horizon against which the best or the good or the most authentic human life can be measured.

Ironically, Luther's very description of sin—"the self turned in upon itself" (*incurvatio in se ipsum*)—implies that the sinful self actually turns in upon itself as a closed system. It turns itself in knots of self-loving and

10. Ibid., 619.

self-loathing. Contemporary Luther scholar Oswald Bayer (1939–) puts it this way:

> The human being, who is made by nature to respond by looking outward, ends up entrapped now in the endless downward spiral of a circle, talking to himself ceaselessly and to those who are like him . . .[11]

The denial of the moral or spiritual element in the human person is, it turns out, close to the heart of what sin *is*—for it is a straight denial that human actions are worthy of a judgement. And it highlights the problem that has dogged the human inward quest since at least the time of Augustine of Hippo in his *Confessions*: that the problem of the self cannot ever be resolved by turning further and further inwards.

That way dragons lie.

There is another paradox that you may have noticed. With Taylor, I lauded "evil" as way of describing human behavior because it actually allows for a great human dignity. It introduces the notion of a responsible agent—a human being answerable for his or her life and so accorded the worth of a being who is capable of change. And yet, on Luther's account, the human person is not so "free." The human will is terribly bound, making the individual a prisoner under the power of sin, tragically unable to do the good they ought to do or even to be the creature it is given them to be. In his marvelous rant *The Bondage of the Will*, Luther wrote:

> Thus the human will is placed between the two like a beast of burden. If God rides it, it wills and goes where God wills . . . If Satan rides it, it wills and goes where Satan wills; nor can it choose to run to either of the two riders or to seek him out, but the riders themselves contend for the possession and control of it.[12]

Luther's critics, the urbane scholar Desiderius Erasmus (1466–1536) among them, have chided him for so demeaning the glory and dignity of man that he should be depicted in such a way. And they have argued that this description is simply deterministic and fatalistic—and that this means the end of ethics. After all, how can appeal to someone to do something when they are simply unable to do it? But at the same time as he spoke so colorfully against the freedom of the will as an illusion, Luther spoke of the way in which this situation was not determined by some distant necessity,

---

11. Bayer, *Martin Luther's Theology*, 183.

12. Luther, "On the Bondage of the Will," 140.

but rather that sin is under the complete ownership of the sinner himself. It is not God who sinned, nor even (from one point of view) the Devil; but it is we who sinned and fell, and it is we who stand in the path of the just wrath of God that is coming on those who rebel. We are the slaves of sin; but as such we are those who put ourselves on the market to be bought. We have the privilege of a judgement on our actions which makes them consequential and meaningful; but also the terrible fear that this judgement might actually be the case.

V FATHER, FATHER

This is Martin Luther's great difficulty, then: *where can I find a gracious God?* Perhaps his own stern, wrathful father didn't help him to see a way of discovering this grace, since he had not experienced it from the old miner. It seemed to him that the Devil and God were in cahoots. They were allied against him in his destruction. The Devil took the holiness and righteousness of God and used it to prove to Luther that due to his woeful performance as a human being, he had no hope of acceptance by God. Even as a monk, Luther could not but perennially doubt how it could be that the face of God was set firmly against him. The way he had been taught about the Christian life was that if human beings were to do whatever it was in them to do, then God would supply the remainder necessary to ensure salvation. And yet it was precisely the precondition of "doing what was in him" (how like a modern self-help manual that sounds!) that the meticulous Luther did not think he could meet. How can I do what is in me when what is in me so compromised?

What then?

Luther had impossible difficulties with the concept of the "righteousness of God." As he understood it initially, it was a divine attribute, or quality—God is just, and that leads him to exercise an impartial judgement of individuals on the basis of their merits (or not). This was very much the Roman lawyer Cicero's (106–43BC) definition of righteousness as "rendering to each person his due."[13] It's balance. Fairness. God in his righteousness gives each individual exactly what they deserve . . .

. . . which is fine if you think human beings are capable of meriting justification. But Luther thought this was simply naïve. He understood human beings as incapable of meeting the preconditions of salvation. They are

13. Cicero, *De Natura Deorum*, III.38.

shot through with sin, bound only for death. They couldn't even get to the start line. And so—how could "the righteousness of God" be anything but bad news for the sinner? God stood frowning and tut-tutting at the end of every corridor.

Was this then the Devil's victory?

Was there no other side to the God that Luther pleaded with in the darkness and loneliness of his room?

We can chart Luther's transformation through the written evidence of his meditations on the Bible. His lecture notes from the period stretching from 1513–1519 are still available. Whether the great insight happened at one sudden, dramatic moment—on the toilet perhaps, who cares?—or over a period of some years is debated by scholars, but it scarcely matters. What Luther came to understand was that the "righteousness of God" included the mercy of God that he shows to sinners despite their sin.

And where can this mercy be found?

Well, it had been under Luther's nose all along; or, at least, it had been pinned to the wall in every room he went. It is in the cross of Jesus Christ. And that is the heart of the concept of "justification." The individual finds himself under the judgement of God, with nowhere to turn, exposed terribly to his wrath. The only place to flee for safety from God's wrath—is to God! And there he finds the treasure of great mercy that lies hidden under the terrible stone of wrath. Christ the crucified one, who suffered on our behalf, became sin for us in order that his righteousness might become our righteousness. The cross shows us in bloody colors God's vehement hostility towards sin; but it also represents (and really is) the depths of the fatherly love of God. If the death of the Son of God shows the extent of the wrath of God against sin, then it comes as a great surprise to realize that it also shows the extent of God's mercy—since it is the Son of God himself who is crucified in such a way.

This takes *faith* to see it for what it is. Or, rather, to *hear* it for what it is. Luther wrote once, "the ears are the organ of the Christian."[14] What he meant was this: faith is simply hearing and believing the message that not only that God is good, but that God is good *to me*. God is good, yes; but that goodness does not spell my destruction but rather my preservation. The Devil's testimony against us is true at a surface level, as the Devil's words often are; but it turns out to have the reality of a lie, since it tempts us to doubt the goodness of God for us, and so to despair.

14. Luther, *Luther's Works*, vol. 29, 224.

The whispered lies of the Devil do not cease once one has begun to have faith. As Luther sees it, the Christian life is lived in the middle of a tension between faith and experience. Our experience very often contradicts our faith. Feelings of guilt, for example, do not leave us automatically, however much we might believe in our own forgiveness. And for many people this is the point at which faith becomes impossible as a personal reality.

This tension between faith and experience was something Luther expounded somewhat later in his career when he thought that he might be martyred by the authorities who were chasing him down. Where was God in this? Has God abandoned me? Luther used the dramatic word *Anfechtung*—"temptation," or "assault"—to describe this experience. The Devil, the world and death are allied in a war against human beings. But surprisingly, this agonizing assault is a work of God too, to reduce the individual to utter reliance on him and him alone. The Devil, it turns out, does God's work without meaning to, because he increases the utter dependence and humility of the believer in the work of God. The absurd, even twisted idea that human beings might help God along a bit is completely thwarted.

Director Woody Allen (1935–) addressed the problem of sin and guilt from this perspective in his film from 1989, *Crimes and Misdemeanors*. The title of the film is doubtless intended to remind us of Dostoyevsky's other great novel, *Crime and Punishment,* which tells the story of the former student Raskolnikov. Raskolnikov commits a horrible and pointless murder but then is unable to live with his conscience and is driven to confess.

In Woody Allen's story, almost the opposite occurs. Judah Rosenthal is a successful and popular optometrist, a family man at the height of his success. His dark secret is that he has a mistress. But when his mistress threatens to expose him to his family, Judah consults his brother who is an organized crime boss. As a result, the mistress is brutally murdered in her home in what is made to look like a robbery. Judah visits her apartment to remove any personal items which could connect him to her, and is appalled to find her bloodied body still lying where it fell.

At first, Allen shows us Judah racked with guilt. It threatens to ruin his life utterly. He is at the point of confessing all because he can't live with himself. He even turns to the religious teachings that he had previously rejected. Now he has the palpable sense that God is watching him and will judge him. However, the chilling conclusion of the film is that time works to soothe his guilt; and eventually, he gets over it. He gets to live his life without his betrayal being exposed to his wife, and his connection to the murder is never traced. He simply ignores the inept spiritualizing of his friend the rabbi and goes on living his triumphant life with its material and domestic pleasures. There is no one to accuse him, ultimately.

Allen lets his audience feel rather conflicted about this, because we do not, most of us, wish to think that murderers can escape without even the burden of a troubled conscience. But on the other hand, we also learn that if the dread of the guilty soul does not actually correspond to a higher reality then we can deal with feelings of guilt as a bad habit bequeathed to us by our religious past. Some people who have lost their faith will often speak of a strange relationship they have with guilt, even in their unbelief. They find that guilty feelings do not dissipate even after God has disappeared for them. Others speak of a sense of relief in leaving guilt behind.

Is that it, then? Most of us do not have the beaten body of our mistresses to haunt our dreams and to tug at our sleeves. But which of us wouldn't rather that death fall on the parts of our lives of which we are ashamed, somewhat like the curtain at the end of a play? At this point, atheism seems rather convenient. If no answering is asked for, none need be given. We can and ought to evolve beyond the feelings of guilt that threaten to spoil our pleasure in life.

And yet: our sense of guilt gives us a dignity—a humanity, even—that the psychoanalyst cannot. It reminds us that we are called to give an answer for our actions. It holds us responsible for them. It won't let us blame our genes or our parents. If we treat our actions and our habits and our feelings towards them as merely biological—healthy or unhealthy rather than right or wrong—we will avoid the truth about them. Our capacity for feeling guilt is like the sensitive skin on our face. It gives us indispensable information about the world and our place in it. And it asks the theological question: if there is to be an accounting for what I do and who I am, then *to whom?* and *when?* And how can I prepare for it?

I would hasten to add that the contemporary diagnosis is not entirely in error: there are forms of guilt that are as tragically crippling as they are unnecessary. On the one hand, it is possible to *feel* guilty for things of which one is patently not guilty. Martin Luther himself was in a sense an example of a person whose feelings of guilt outstripped his moral and spiritual reality. In our time, it has been frequently observed that victims of abuse experience feelings of guilt even though they are not the perpetrators of the abuse. On the other hand, it could be that guilt adheres to a person's sexual feelings, even when these are in every sense completely in the range

of normality. Of all social forces, religion is associated with a kind of illegitimate fostering of guilt within people. But that guilt has its distorted
forms, or that we are not good at self-diagnosing these feelings, does not
mean that guilt *per se* is not an extremely useful human sensation.

VI BINDING THE STRONG MAN

Luther was a medieval man inhabiting a world vastly different from ours—
a world in which it surprised no one to think that a being like the Devil
might stalk the halls and hide in cupboards. We find that altogether too
lurid. But perhaps we are too readily thrown by Luther's talk of the Devil
and miss the deep human truth that is exposed in his spiritual experience.

That truth relates to the problem of guilt and the possibility that we
stand accused before a final court. The real spiritual shift that has taken
place in the last century and a half is not so much to do with the question
of metaphysical beings like angels and devils but to do with the state of the
human heart. The challenge to the existence of the God of Luther (and of
Paul, and of Jesus Christ) means the end of any prospect of an ultimate
judgement on human behaviours and attitudes. What is truly significant
about this, as we have already seen, is that the notion of guilt has gone from
being a reality attended by certain unpleasant feelings to simply a neurosis,
or a feeling associated with eating fatty foods. The human experience of
guilt has become a sickness that is need of a therapeutic solution and is not
now a moral problem.

Given the track record of people like Jim Jones (1931–78), whose followers killed themselves *en masse* by taking poisoned Kool-Aid in 1978, it
is not unreasonable to ask the question of any charismatic religious leader
with a following "are you working here for good, or for ill? For God, or for
someone else?" So it is unsurprising to learn that Jesus of Nazareth was
himself accused by his contemporaries of being in league with Satan. Especially when people heard of his activity as an exorcist, they seemed to
think that this was an indication of an alliance with a sinister power. Mark's
Gospel records that his family thought he was out of his mind, and that the
teachers of the law claimed that he was utilizing the power of the prince of
demons to drive out demons.

Jesus's words in response are characteristically teasing:

> How can Satan drive out Satan? If a kingdom is divided against
> itself, that kingdom cannot stand. If a house is divided against

itself, that house cannot stand. And if Satan opposes himself and is divided, he cannot stand; his end has come. In fact, no one can enter a strong man's house without first tying him up. Then he can plunder the strong man's house. (Mark 3:23b–27)

Just say, says Jesus, I *am* an agent of the Devil himself. If the demons are fleeing before the prince of demons himself, then it seems that they are in the grip of some bizarre demonic civil war. In which case: this is good news! The end has come for him.

But of course Jesus is not in league with the Devil. That's the point of the "strong man" idea. You can't take someone's stuff unless your power excels his. If Jesus is burgling Beelzebub (which means releasing people from his power), he must be both opposed to the accuser, and more powerful than the accuser.

The final and most devastating satanic lie is this: that you are guilty and that there is nothing beyond that terrible conclusion. His spiritual power is to hold human beings in despair. Many once-religious people have come to the conclusion that they cannot live with this feeling of dread. And, as I said above: many religious groups have introduced distorted forms of guilt as a problem into the human psyche and then offered nothing that would free the individual from it. This is religion at its most satanic.

And yet that is to miss the essence of Jesus's work for human beings— that he at once takes us with the utmost seriousness as moral agents *and* makes possible a release from the devastating consequences of the things we do.

⊗

One of the great satanic weapons is, as we have seen, despair. This hopelessness is a *timed* condition: that is, it is an anti-faith about what our prospects are in regard to the future. We can see time as it passes, but we cannot really do more than observe. In the next chapter, then, I will ask concerning our life in time and explore the way faith intersects with it and changes it.

FOUR

The Patience of Faith

Time, the gourmet, sees that the objects of this world have been ripened by the
fire of the sun, and when he finds them fully ripe he consumes them!

YOGA VASISTHA[1]

I THE TIME OF OUR LIVES

There is no other way of living life other than within time. We are reminded
of this constantly, in the technological paradise in which we live, because
we are surrounded with clocks. We have put time-pieces in every machine
we own as if to say to them "we are time-bound; you machines should share
our condition." But even without these time machines, our bodies themselves remind us how time-bound we are. We grow and then we decline;
and we are never *not* either growing or declining.

There was a time when this observation was used by poets to do what
poets have always done: seduce women. So, Andrew Marvell (1621–78)
writing "to his coy mistress" penned the memorable couplet

> But at my back I always hear
> Time's winged chariot hurrying near.[2]

1. Hindu text, dated between eleventh and fourteenth centuries AD.
2. Marvell, "To His Coy Mistress," 186–87.

His playful theme is this: the woman's shyness in refusing his advances and preserving her chastity is a failure to see how short the time is for the lovers. Indeed, the alluring glow of her young skin, like the dew of the morning, is a sign of just how temporary bodily life is. There is no stilling the onward march of time; there is only the chance to enjoy life's pleasures while they are on offer. The seductive power of the poem is the way in which Marvell takes the rather serious idea of the passing of time and human mortality and cheekily offers it as a gambit in his own bedroom politics. It's a serious joke, and you assume it all comes to a lusty conclusion.

We don't do poems quite like that anymore. Perhaps the ladies to whom such poems are addressed have heard it all before. But idea that time is passing for human beings even as they think about it still fascinates poets. The English poet Philip Larkin (1922–85) did not write big philosophical books with grand-sounding titles like *Being and Time.* That was not his way. Yet he compressed a great deal of profundity into his small, plain-speaking poems. One of the themes that interested him most was the passing of time—not in a grand historical sense, but in the sense of the passing of an ordinary human life.

> What are days for?
> Days are where we live.
> They come, they wake us
> Time and time over.
> They are to be happy in:
> Where can we live but days?[3]

Days are not like some cul-de-sac laced suburb in which we can purchase a nice piece of real estate. We cannot live anywhere else. Here we are, living in them. They are the base fact of our life: there is no point contesting them. You might as well find a way to be happy in your days.

But Larkin has a second stanza to add to this first:

> Ah, solving that question
> Brings the priest and the doctor
> In their long coats
> Running over the fields.[4]

This is faintly satirical, or at least a little barbed. The priest and the doctor are the great explainers, the great question solvers who rush with as much

3. Larkin, "Days," *Collected Poems.*
4. Ibid.

haste as they can summon to make us think we can live somewhere else other than in "days." This, Larkin appears to saying, is futile. There is no answer to the question "where can we live but days?" but "nowhere." Or, there is no "answer," because getting to the point of asking the question is in fact the insight that the poet wants us to grasp.

Though these poems and their authors couldn't be more different, they are both interested in the connection between human happiness and the human experience of time. We have days, says Larkin, "to be happy in." Marvell reminds his mistress that there isn't a lot of lovemaking happening in the coldness of the tomb: pleasure has to take place within a particular living moment. The rather crass but perfectly true equation is this: if you have no moments, you can have no pleasure.

Larkin was not always so upbeat about the time of human living. If days were to be happy in, then this rumination from his later poem "Dockery and Son" reveals how allusive this happiness was to him:

> Life is first boredom, then fear.
> Whether or not we use it, it goes,
> And leaves what something hidden from us chose,
> And age, and then the only end of age.[5]

"The only end of age": death, whose forerunner is the physical decay and illness of old age. Boredom and fear might seem an odd coupling. On the one hand, the bored person cannot think what to do with the time. And yet that is the overture to an anxiety about losing time—a fear of what may happen as one approaches the pain, suffering, and oblivion that we all inevitably face. Larkin teases us with his mysterious, fatalistic reference to a "something hidden from us" that chooses the things that are to be left from our lives. There is some blind and inaccessible force beyond us that marks our times—whether the grinding mechanism of cause and effect or some quasi-divine force like fate, we are unsure. Whatever it is, the effect is the same: a feeling of complete impotence as we see the past freezing behind us, and the number of our days to come rapidly falling.

Mostly we keep the persistent drumbeat of time at bay by orchestrating over it a symphony of frenetic activity. Strange to say, it is those ordinary moments when we lose control of our daily timetables that our life-in-time becomes most present to us. When we wait on a busy street for an overdue bus, or become trapped in a lengthy meeting which is badly managed, we

5. Larkin, "Dockery and Son," *Collected Poems.*

are pulled unwillingly out of our forgetfulness about the value and meaning of time. And we have our lack of control over time thrust in our faces—our inability to summon the bus, or to know why it is late is just a refraction to us in a particular moment of our inability to reconcile ourselves to time.

Let me take you to one of those work meetings in which time seems to bank up like water before a damn. It's the usual kind of thing: starting at 2 p.m. with the possibility of stretching long into the afternoon; people in chairs around a table sighing into their instant coffees. What kind of experience is it? As a member of the meeting you instantly recognize that the agenda is dominated by administrivia that is inaccessible except to those who have specialist knowledge and a perverse interest. The interjections of some individuals are liable to derail the process and lengthen the session to no productive end. Issues that have been discussed for years keep re-emerging. You know as a relatively junior member of the team that your opinion isn't really wanted in any case.

And so, there you are, as the clock ticks ever on. The feelings you experience are by turns frustration, anxiety, disappointment, and regret. You mull over the things you could be doing with the time—the lost opportunities for making progress on your projects, the deadlines that you have looming, even the chance to perhaps go home a little early and play with your children. You doodle on your notepad. You check your emails and compose responses—which is a small redemption of the time at least. You poke someone on Facebook (which is *so*, like, 2008).

Inwardly, though, you are dying. You are transfixed by a kind of social norm which says that it is rude simply to walk out without a reasonable excuse. The meeting ticks around into its third hour, and you start to become physically uncomfortable. Long ago, you lost the thread of the meeting, and you feebly assent to whatever proposals are put forward without really caring, even though these will have an impact on your workplace. You have ascended to that plane where you simply don't care anymore. What you *are* aware of is the time that is passing—and it is agonizing to watch.

Why does it feel this way? These time traps are certainly features of contemporary life, where we can point to the plethora of alternative options in any given moment as to how we could make use of the time. At every point, we could be doing what we are doing *or* something else. It is infuriating to lose that choice. A more simple lifestyle would not have the options, but would not have the lobster pots of time into which we seem to crawl so often either: the computer malfunction, the traffic snafu, the cancelled flight.

But it isn't simply the loss of options. It's the loss of control, on the one hand; and the reminder that our time is finite, on the other: these things make the experience of the time trap so unbearable. There doesn't seem to be a purpose to the time being spent, and yet time isn't pausing for us while we discover one. It simply goes.

Our consciousness of time's passing in one of the things that makes us human—for we are able to lock the past in language like a bug in amber, and we are able to give voice to our dreams. We are aware of the past and the future in ways that we find it hard to imagine that the other creatures are. A tree keeps a count of the years in its trunk, but is not aware of its own age. It is impossible to think of a dog caring whether you forgot its birthday or not, even though we pet-owners like to throw them presents and sing to them (or is that just me?).

But at the same time as we can be conscious of the past and the future because we can talk about them, we also find them tantalizingly out of reach. It is always possible to dispute the past of our experience because all we have is our experience of it—which may turn out to be mistaken. A friend of mine came home to visit his parents one day when he was in his twenties only to have his mother announce that she had been having an affair with a family friend for more than a decade, and was now moving out with him. The trauma this caused him was not least because the memories he had of happy family holidays with this family friend were no longer what they had seemed to be at the time. His experience in the first place was a faulty or incomplete experience of what had in fact occurred—and now, knowing the truth, he could not possess that memory as it once had been. This was an unusual experience, it has to be said. But the possibility that something like this could occur puts a question mark against our precious relationship to the past.

Furthermore, it is not exactly a revelation to observe that we can't change the past however much we would like to. We can perhaps change the historical record, or tell untruths about the past. But we know that can't change it really: what has happened lies sealed in the road behind us. The past is completely unforgiving about our regrets and mistakes.

The future is out of reach in a different way. It is this way simply because of what we all know: that it is unknown. What we do know from our experience of the world is this: that there are forces in the world and in human society that are simply greater than we are, and which we cannot predict, or that it is useless to predict. We are simply unaware, other than as a possibility, of what drunk driver will meet us on the road, or what tumor will grow in our bodies, or what the economy will do to our livelihoods, or what declaration of war will completely alter the fabric of our daily lives. The most prepared we can be is to be prepared for the unpredictable. The great Australian novelist David Malouf (1934–) writes:

> What most alarms us in our contemporary world, what unsettles and scares us, is the extent to which the forces that shape our lives are no longer personal—they know nothing of us; and to the extent that we know nothing of them—cannot put a face to them, cannot find in them anything we recognize as human—we cannot deal with them. We feel like small, powerless creatures in the coils of an invisible monster, vast but insubstantial, that cannot be grasped or wrestled with.[6]

As the poets have noted, our uncertainty about the future deeply affects our ability to be happy with the lives we have. The more thoughtful we are, the more aware we are that any happiness we experience is only momentary, and dependent upon factors that may unexpectedly change. Our prosperity can be eroded; our relatives taken from us. Could this be the reason that people in the prosperous West are very reluctant to admit to feeling satisfied, despite the fact that they live much more secure lives than anyone ever has before?

Not without justification we could say that our consciousness—and in our era, our hyper-consciousness—of time passing is a curse. We could read it as one of those Greek myths, where a great gift has been given to a mortal by the gods but with a key facet of the gift missing, so that it turns into a terrible burden. Tithonus, for example, is given the gift of immortality, but is not prevented from aging. In the end he longs for death as a mercy, but he cannot die. So human beings have consciousness of time but have to watch it bearing down on them, like the cinematic cliché of the person tied to the railway tracks in front of a steam train. We know it is approaching, but what good does knowing it do?

Arguably, we are at our happiest when we are least aware of time. When we are absorbed in an activity to the degree that we no longer notice time passing, we achieve a state that the U.S. psychologist Mihály

---

6. Malouf, "The Happy Life," 55.

Csíkszentmihályi (1934–) calls "flow."[7] Our concentration is focused into a singular moment; and we are able to forget about the demands that time makes upon us. In those places in which challenge corresponds to skill, the anxieties of the unknown future slip into the periphery of our consciousness. All we are aware of is the task at hand—hitting the ball over the net, playing the piece of music, giving the speech, meditating. Conversely, depression and anxiety block off an individual's access to the state of flow—which unfortunately makes depression and anxiety worse.

II THE LONGSUFFERING

In what ways has our time-consciousness had an impact on faith in God? Or perhaps we need to acknowledge the possibility that our culture's declining faith in God has had an impact on our time-consciousness. The relationship is complex and recursive. Samuel Beckett's (1906–89) famous play *Waiting for Godot* (premiered 1953) makes a kind of dark fun at the futile hopes of its characters. The plot is perfectly simple: two men named Vladimir and Estragon make the audience laugh while waiting for someone called "Godot" who never appears. Despite Beckett's protests that Godot was not meant to be thought of as "God," the biblical and religious echoes in the play are very suggestive of a theological concern. The play is fairly slathered in allusions from scripture, including an intriguing discussion of the thief on the cross. Godot is said to keep sheep and goats, which sounds very much like the biblical divinity. But even without these, simply by setting up a narrative Beckett is pointing to the way we, out of habit, conceive of time as consisting of a beginning, middle, and an end. When we have a beginning, we expect an end. By not offering us one—and yet by keeping his audience entertained for the full length of the play—Beckett is saying something deeply disturbing: that our sense of an ending is perhaps simply a layer we place upon the events of our experience. Perhaps passing the time is more important and of more significance than what we are passing the time *for*. Hope—especially the hope claimed by a biblical faith—is a distraction.

The Christian tradition has always spoken of the return of Jesus Christ. The early Christians prayed *marana tha* (come, O Lord!). Christianity has always had an *eschatology*, in other words, something to say about the end of all things; and Christians have since earliest times given voice to a hope

7. Csíkszentmihályi, *Flow*.

not only that things will get better over time, but that there will be a decisive conclusion to time. One of the difficulties of this doctrine in the history of Christianity is that the scriptural language describing the last things is stretched as far as it will go by symbol and metaphor. Insensitivity to the nature of the language the Bible authors used to describe the things that are far beyond our experience has led at various times to crass speculations and pseudo-prophetic movements led by would-be messiah figures. As a reaction to this feature of Christianity especially in its popular forms, some scholars since the Enlightenment have described a Christianity shorn of its eschatological elements. For D. F. Strauss (1808–74), author of *Leben Jesu* (1835), Jesus was an apocalyptic prophet who simply got it wrong—an error repeated by the early church. His real value for today is as a romantic vision of liberal humanity at its finest. There was thus for Strauss the possibility of Christianity-*sans*-eschatology—especially in the ethical teaching of Christ.

So we can see already within the camp of Christianity a move to scrub away the embarrassment of these apparently primitive eschatological elements. God is not coming to end history and bring time to its conclusion—that language in the Bible was said to be a myth entirely encapsulated in the history of Jesus of Nazareth. The historian Ernst Troeltsch (1865–1923) wrote in an essay entitled "The Significance of the Historical Existence of Jesus for Faith":

> When it first formed its religious ides the primitive Christian community had already taken Jesus out of history and made him Logos and God, the eternal Christ appearing to us in historical form, one who is related in essence to the eternal Godhead and so not unnaturally the object of faith. But historical criticism, grown up in a world no longer dominated by the church, has returned him to history where all is finite and conditioned.[8]

Contemporary criticism of the Bible had swept away, in Troeltsch's view, all the unnecessary accretions of church dogma with all its talk of the eternal God and of the world to come, and opened up the possibility for a new consideration of Jesus as simply a historical figure. This was typical of theology of the early twentieth century. As the German theologian Jürgen Moltmann (1926–), a critic of this turn, has said:

---

8. Troeltsch, *Ernst Troeltsch*, 182.

> For modern theology the early Christian expectation of the par-
> ousia is an embarrassment which it thinks it can get rid of with the
> help of demythologization.[9]

Popular level Christianity, as if in direct defiance of the scholarly guild, has featured wilder and wilder predictions about the future return of Christ—most crassly exemplified by the bafflingly best-selling *Left Behind* series that were published in the 1980s and 90s in the U.S.

However, the loss of an expectation of God's return at the conclusion of history parallels an increased sense of disillusionment with and even anger toward a God who apparently refuses to act against evil in the world. We can see this in *Waiting for Godot*: Beckett isn't simply laughing at poor deluded theists with a smug sense of superiority. The unbelief that comes through in the play is a more believing unbelief than that. The feelings of disappointment or rage against the God who remained absent and silent in the face of the horrors and savagery of the twentieth century is magnified by the loss of belief in the God "who is to come." If his promise to intervene is disregarded, then it seems we have more grounds to complain against him for not intervening.

The protest against God's inaction wouldn't have any force against a God who was absolutely non-existent. If he does not exist, then you are wasting your breath complaining about him from the start; and your emotional energy is better held in reserve. But what has been lost is a God who is not merely a benign force but is also the Lord of history. That is: the version of Christianity frequently rejected, by apathy as much as by active non-belief, is a Christianity shorn of the God to whom the psalmist prays "my times are in your hand." Against this emaciated view of God there is a justified protest, for he is impotent at best, a maker of false promises at worst.

We are left abandoned by God in the middle of history. We have nothing to do but to nurse our suffering, to curse him for gifting us with a consciousness of time that prompts us to hope for a meaningful conclusion to history where there is none. It is simply an unfortunate by-product of the evolution of our brains. Our experience of suffering then becomes not simply one of pain, but one of despair. Our suffering is intensified by our awareness that there is no future, or only the prospect of a bleak one; our happiness is compromised by it.

---

9. Moltmann, *The Way of Jesus Christ*, 313.

That we exist within time is a hidden aspect of the traditional debates about the problem of suffering and evil. We experience evil and suffering as deeply problematic in relation to faith in God because on the one hand we have the expectation of Beckett's audience that a beginning will lead to an end, and on the other we cannot envisage a "solution" or a "remedy" occurring within the span of life we have to lead. Three score years and ten is the length by which we tend to measure time; that we have this habit is evidence merely of the framing of all our experiences by our bodily existence in the world.

And yet the writers of scripture know this already. It is remarkable how the debate about the problem of evil goes on as if the Bible knows nothing of it at all—as if the Bible were written from a great height. But suffering and evil are deeply troubling to the writers of what we call the "Word of God." They write not from some point of eternity, but in the midst of time. History swirls around them as they work. They record genocide, murder, tyranny, and rape. They tell of the exploitation of the poor and the desecration of sacred spaces. They know what it is like to call out "my God, my God, why?" They plead with God to make good his claim to sovereignty over history and to moral purity and goodness. The Bible is a messy book, stained with the many tears of its authors who wept not only over the sins of the people of God but also with bewilderment at God's inaction.

This isn't the whole story of course: the Bible is, at the same time as it is a recognition of the sense of bewilderment at God's absence and inaction, also a testimony to God's active presence and his promise to come again. A faith such as the one we encounter in the pages of the Bible is not going to be a belief that pretends that evil and suffering don't exist. Neither is biblical faith the sort of faith that minimizes the impact of suffering by saying something glib like "it'll all work out in the end."

This is the difficulty with the two standard defenses against the problem of evil traditionally offered by Christians—Augustine of Hippo's "free-will" defense, and Irenaeus of Lyons' (c. 130–202) "soul-making" defence. Augustine (in very brief) argued that the good of giving us free will outweighed the bad of having us harm each other and suffer harm. The Irenaean argument (likewise in very brief) claims that suffering and evil are necessary in some way to human moral development—a process that is at the present time unfinished. Both of these arguments involve us in making the highly problematic claim that God intends to bring about a good by means of evil and suffering. Even though Augustine could see the problem with making evil something necessary for the ultimate good, it is hard to see how his theodicy escapes this problem. The pastoral problem this argument causes highlights just how inadequate it is. If you have heard a well-meaning relative say to a teenager whose father has just been killed in car accident on a distant country road "God has some higher purpose in this" (as I have) you'll know what I mean.

Irenaeus's solution at least has the advantage of pointing us towards an unseen future. Some ultimate purpose justifies this penultimate experience of pain, in this view. This is something like the biblical answer, though the Bible writers don't attempt the justification. How the Bible addresses evil and suffering does not amount to a justification for them, as if they are necessary to the whole plan of the universe—as if the creation *included* the fall already within it. That line of thought leaves us with a monstrous God, or none at all. The Bible simply recognizes the existence of evil and suffering and turns us to the character of God, which is revealed to us in what he does in history to make himself a people and live in a loving proximity to them.

III STILL WAITING

One of the features of the faith which we find expressed in scripture is the way it is linked to the virtue of *patience*. Israel learnt how to wait for God. Such was the only right (indeed righteous) response to a God who makes promises. Abraham—so often the exemplar of biblical faith!—made false steps in this regard, taking Hagar for his substitute wife in his impatience. Waiting for God, it turns out, means enduring the experience of that which is contrary to his promise—the rise of the enemy, the non-appearance of the promised child, living outside the land, and so on.[10] In particular, it was that period known as the Exile—when the Babylonians conquered Jerusalem and took her citizens into captivity—that evoked the call to wait: to endure the time of penitence and await the coming of the Lord in redemption. Take Psalm 130:

> Out of the depths I cry to you, O LORD.
> Lord, hear my voice! Let your ears be attentive to the voice of my supplications!
> If you, O LORD, should mark iniquities, Lord, who could stand?
> But there is forgiveness with you, so that you may be revered.

10. We'll meet Abraham again in Chapter 6.

> I wait for the LORD, my soul waits, and in his word I hope;
> my soul waits for the Lord more than those who watch for the
> morning, more than those who watch for the morning.
> O Israel, hope in the LORD! For with the LORD there is steadfast
> love, and with him is great power to redeem.
> It is he who will redeem Israel from all its iniquities.

Faith in the promises of God corresponds to God's own characteristic steadfastness—his transcendence of time by his self-constancy. He has "steadfast love." The Hebrew word *hesed,* which this translates, combines the enduring with the personal. God's endurance is not simply remorseless and unchanging, but has the quality of love. It has an object, that is to say: the people whom he loves.

Israel had long borne witness to that quality in God. But with the Exile came a sense of longing for a now-absent God to come, in the person of the Messiah: a God-sent person who will restore the fortunes of hapless Israel by defeating her enemies and returning her to the land once lost. The prophet Isaiah spoke about the consolation of Israel that was in this hope, for it meant that the tears of despair would be wiped away.

For the prophets Simeon and Anna and for faithful Israel, the wait is over when the boy Jesus arrives. But Jesus's coming to Israel also begins a new period of waiting. His ascension and the expectation of his return underpin New Testament faith. The risen Lord now rules in heaven, but rules unseen and absent. His absence is necessary for the era of the proclamation of the gospel to the nations. His disciples wait in Jerusalem until the Spirit is given to them at Pentecost to empower the public declaration of the message. Like Old Testament faith, New Testament faith needs the key virtue of *hupomones*, or "patient endurance," in order to withstand not only the prolonged absence of the Lord but the presence of trials and tests in the present evil age. A passage like this from 2 Peter is representative:

> But do not ignore this one fact, beloved, that with the Lord one
> day is like a thousand years, and a thousand years are like one day.
> The Lord is not slow about his promise, as some think of slowness,
> but is patient with you, not wanting any to perish, but all to come
> to repentance. . . . But, in accordance with his promise, we wait
> for new heavens and a new earth, where righteousness is at home.
> Therefore, beloved, while you are waiting for these things,
> strive to be found by him at peace, without spot or blemish; and
> regard the patience of our Lord as salvation. (2 Pet 3:8–9, 13–15a)

In the biblical book of Hebrews, famous letter of endurance and perseverance, faith is given this eschatological edge to it: faith is "the assurance of things hoped for, the conviction of things not seen" (11:1). The faith of the ancients was exemplary because by it they were able to endure all sorts of trials.

The Christian waits. But she is busy with waiting—active in resisting sin and in doing good works. Her waiting is a waiting for the risen and ascended Lord to judge the earth and to vindicate the elect. It is a waiting for the apocalypse—for the final revelation of things hidden from view. Waiting means allowing that the decisive world-ending action will be God's in Christ—that the building of utopian visions of humankind on earth is not for now. Waiting means resisting the powers and authorities where they counter Christ's ultimate authority, and serving them insofar as they reflect it.

Meditating on his own failing sight, the great poet John Milton (1608–74) dictated this sonnet, "On His Blindness":

> When I consider how my light is spent,
> Ere half my days in this dark world and wide,
> And that one talent which is death to hide
> Lodged with me useless, though my soul more bent
> To serve therewith my Maker, and present
> My true account, lest He returning chide;
> "Doth God exact day-labor, light denied?"
> I fondly ask. But Patience, to prevent
> That murmur, soon replies, "God doth not need
> Either man's work or His own gifts. Who best
> Bear His mild yoke, they serve Him best. His state
> Is kingly: thousands at His bidding speed,
> And post o'er land and ocean without rest;
> They also serve who only stand and wait.

The poem adds another dimension to the Christian posture towards time. Even physical enfeeblement does not prevent the believer from serving God truly, since the nature of this service is a patient endurance in any case. Suffering is not denied or minimized in human experience by this faith—how could it be when its central symbol is a man dying on a bloody cross? But faith enables the believer to put suffering in the context of hope. What is now will not be then.

This relates to our prospects for happiness, too. Without hope, all we can say for happiness is that we should grasp it while we have it and not think about it too much lest we talk ourselves out of it. In the world of suffering—our own, and others'—we can only really say that we are at our most happy when we are least aware of the way things are. Yet the New Testament makes some shocking statements about this, such as this one from James: "Consider it pure joy . . . when you suffer all kinds of trials" (1:2). How is this even a meaningful thing to say (unless it is commanding a form of masochism)?

It makes sense because with faithful hope—the patience of faith—we can experience happiness in the midst of suffering as *joy*. Hope turns happiness into joy. The joy is not *despite* the sufferings, but actually *in* them. This is not because of some perversity, but because the sufferings themselves are part of a wider context. The sufferings of the persecuted Christians were not somehow "good" in and of themselves, but they were evidence of the lashing out of the forces of evil against the providence of the good God. Suffering in this way does not compromise joy in the way that it inevitably gate-crashes happiness.

But without a real expectation of the God who is to come in time, it is not possible to produce this effect. You cannot have a kind of pseudo-faith in a non-religious religion without hope other than in the human spirit, despite what Alain de Botton says in his book *Religion for Atheists*. You cannot observe the happiness of religious people, and then suggest that we take the practices of religion without the beliefs in order to achieve the same effect. This kind of "faith" is as liable to fretting about time as no faith at all.

Our discussion of faith has thus far addressed the chiefly existential difficulties of faith—our experiences of love, loss and death, the unbearable weight of our moral inadequacies, the situation of our existence in time. But in Christianity faith is not simply a kind of existence, or an attitude towards existing. There are things which faith claims to know. There are knowledge claims bound up with faith. It is to the state of knowledge that we now turn.

FIVE

Living in the World of Experts

An expert is someone who knows some of the worst mistakes, which can be made, in a very narrow field.

NIELS BOHR, PHYSICIST

I KNOWLEDGE IS POWER

It is not a novelty to observe that "knowledge is power"—Sir Francis Bacon (1561–1626) epigrammed it sometime in the seventeenth century. But it is one of those truths that has become somehow more true since it was first uttered. In an age in which information is thought of as the one thing most worth having, *knowledge*—which implies being able to get something useful out of all that data—becomes a priceless commodity. Billions of dollars have changed hands for the right to own knowledge.

But this has become one of the most overwhelming aspects of contemporary life. The sheer volume of information that I can readily access is completely overwhelming. The Internet has, it goes without saying, intensified this feeling many times over. How can you know anything when there is so much to know? And if knowledge is power, and the one thing I know is how much I don't know, then it is pretty disempowering, isn't it? The mystique of Google is in part due to the way in which it has mastered the organization, calibration, and delivery of knowledge, and (perhaps most of all) made it saleable. It is a triaging of knowledge.

And so, we turn to the experts.

An expert is a person who we recognize as having a very high degree of knowledge or skill in a particular area. Experts would usually have both experience and learning combined. For example, an airline pilot is not only someone who knows how to fly an Airbus. He (it is most often a he) has also recorded several thousand flying hours at the helm of a commercial passenger jet. Usually, the expert pilot has the experience of being the co-pilot to a more experienced pilot, so that he can gain the experience he needs.

What's more, the airline pilot, like other experts, has a license to fly that is given to him by the statutory authorities. A person may or may not be skilled and knowledgeable in some area, but if he or she is not recognized to be such, his or her expertise may be useless. An unlicensed pilot simply does not get to fly an Airbus 330, unless he is involved in some terrorist action. (And, by the way, airlines have made sure that they never have to make an announcement to the passengers like "does anyone know how to fly a plane?") The point is: recognition is vital, because it conveys the authority and status to the expert that is needed to operate as an expert. There is a social dimension to expertise, in other words.

We have a number of social institutions that are set up in order to recognize expertise so that we ordinary folks can quickly and with confidence place our trust in the hands of the expert. The professional guild is a group of experts whose job is to recognize the expertise of others and admit them to its number. Governments have regulatory authorities which combine peer assessment with the development of bureaucratic criteria which help mediate to the public the expertise of the expert. These bodies can have the power to disendorse the expert by removing his or her credentials.

Imagine that I need to see a brain surgeon because (heaven forbid) a tumor has been discovered growing in my brain and I am having terrible headaches. I turn up to my appointment at the right time only to discover that the surgery is in a very seedy part of town, that the receptionist is grumpy and sits at her desk painting her toenails, and that the magazines in the waiting room are several years old. When I meet Dr. Mort—an unpromising name for a surgeon—I notice that he has very shaky hands, bloodshot eyes, and the faint whiff of alcohol on his breath. But I do notice that on his wall he has qualifications from the best schools of brain surgery. And my GP, who I have been seeing for years, has warmly recommended Dr. Mort as a fine brain surgeon.

The concept of expert knowledge is functioning here on a number of levels. In the first place, I have no idea even about how I would go about measuring the expertise of a person who called himself a brain surgeon for myself. My degrees in English and theology just won't stack up. I simply could not with any credibility stand in judgement over the various aspects of brain surgery—unless there are rather obvious facts on the table, such as a pattern of terrible deaths. Dr. Mort does not make a favorable first impression, to be sure. He won't make eye contact, and he constantly checks his emails while I am talking to him. But his qualifications and the recommendation of my doctor testify loudly that this man is a very good choice for me to make in determining which doctor I want to cut the top of my head off and poke around inside. In fact, as he is a brain surgeon in good standing with the relevant government authorities and ultimately accountable to them, most people would be inclined to trust him without too much reflection. The whole system of trust in expertise operates as a kind of social shorthand, meaning that the time-consuming and inaccessible research is done for us already. In the case of the airline pilot, we don't think it strange that we never meet or even learn the name of the person in whose hands we happily place our lives. We just take it as a given that the person up the front wearing a peaked cap is expert enough to fly 12,000 meters high at several hundred kilometers an hour for several hours, possibly in the dark.

Uniforms are another way in which a social convention helps us to recognize expertise. A uniform conveys authority and status on a particular person in such a way that it can be instantly recognized. We really only consider the way in which this happens when someone uses the convention to take advantage of us. But this is really evidence that, in the overwhelming majority of cases, the convention works very well. In a crowded railway station looking for the toilets, I instantly look for a person who is wearing a railway employee's uniform. At a restaurant, a waiter will indicate his or her status to act as a waiter by carrying a white cloth—or even by subtle gestures and body language. Traveling on an overnight ferry recently I approached a lady who was wearing a lanyard around her neck and asked her what time the onboard cinema was showing its first film. It turned out that she was simply a member of the public—and the lanyard, had I inspected it more closely, contained nothing that would indicate that she was a steward at all.

What would we do without experts? We rely on them to fix our cars, to give us financial advice, to heal our bodies, to manage our diets, and to tell us that the computer is completely kaput because of the faulty motherboard—which I didn't know I had until mine broke. Our dependence on the experts is endemic. We can't begin to operate in any meaningful way in our über-urban high-tech environment without the assistance of those who really know what they are talking about. Do-it-yourself is dead: the idea that I might fix my own car, for example, is now passé. There's far too much complex gadgetry beneath the hood for that. And that's why we are so indebted to expert knowledge.

The extraordinary exploits of conman Frank Abagnale, Jr. (1948–) were made into the film *Catch Me if You Can,* directed by Stephen Spielberg in 2002. Before he was even nineteen years old, Abagnale had managed to inveigle his way onto over two hundred fifty Pan American flights and traveled to twenty-six countries. His method? He impersonated an airline pilot complete with uniform and "deadheaded," which is when airline staff are ferried free of charge to meet flights that they subsequently work on. Abagnale claimed that pilots frequently offered him the controls of the plane, and that once he actually flew an aircraft for a brief period at 30,000 feet. He said later that he was "very much aware that I had been handed custody of 140 lives, my own included . . . because I couldn't fly a kite." He also impersonated a doctor and served as a resident pediatrician in a Georgia hospital; and took the Louisiana bar exam so that he could work for the Attorney General's office in that state. Abagnale's confidence tricks relied on the huge faith that we place in experts and the readiness with which we trust them. We are practiced at believing them, and we know that life goes more smoothly when we just do. In performing his remarkable feats of impersonating experts, Abagnale of course earned himself the authority of an expert in security and fraud, and has made a very nice living since his release from prison as a security consultant.

The spread of the cult of expertise is a feature of a highly specialized and high-tech economic system. This is in contrast to pre-industrialized societies in which most people would function as subsistence farmers; and even in contrast to many industrialized systems where a great number of people work in factories in which there may be specialized skills but not many of those regarded as "expert." The post-World War II prosperity and the silicon revolution of the 1970s have combined to ensure that Western people aspire to careers in which highly specialized skills and an in-depth education are necessary. Many of us spend years of our lives becoming experts—a process that takes hard work and focused study, but which is rewarded by the recognition of our society that we have authority in our area. The economic value of higher education is a measure of nothing less than the importance of knowledge in the psyche of Western individuals. Our expertise is a commodity we can sell in order to gain access to the advice of other experts. And one should not underestimate the importance of this factor: it helps us feel proud at dinner parties when people ask "what do you do?"

The most observant—if not the most lucid—of social critics of expert knowledge was the French philosopher Michel Foucault (1926–84). He created several wonderful neologisms in an effort to describe how knowledge and power mutually constitute one another in human societies and especially in the modern era. It was in *Discipline and Punish,* his work on the practice of judicial punishment in the modern era, that Foucault observed the way in which gathering, analyzing and ultimately *knowing* information about people could be an instrument in changing their behavior.[1] The prison systems that developed in Western nations during the nineteenth century employed a series of "professionals"—psychologists, criminologists, medical officers, and so on—who were given power over the prisoner which was exercised not by brute force but simply by observing and categorizing behaviors. This was what Foucault labeled "power/knowledge." And as far as he was concerned, what occurs in prisons lies on a continuum with the rest of society. He noted resemblances between the various institutions of social control—schools, the military, psychiatric institutions, and hospitals—and described the way in which a culture of behavior is inculcated in these merely by the collecting and reporting of information by people who have formed themselves into professional guilds—each of which accrues to itself an aura of authority and status.

Think of how difficult it is to resist the word of an expert. I recall myself once talking my small son, then about a year old, to the casualty ward of the local hospital with a persistent high temperature. When after several hours we were admitted to the hospital itself "for observation" it was clear that whatever the ailment was, it was very minor. But the regime of the hospital demanded that he be kept in overnight. When we went up

1. Foucault, *Discipline and Punish.*

onto the ward, the scene of chaos which greeted us was very distressing: another small child had just emerged from an operation on his leg and was being attended to by at least ten relatives—some of them also upset, some of them simply talking very loudly to each other. It took all the willpower at my disposal (as a person who normally conforms to social expectations) to demand of the hospital staff that we be allowed to take our son home to his own bed. The series of release forms I then had to sign were clearly designed to intimidate me as much as possible by reminding me of my own amateurism. And yet: I was certainly making the right decision.

But Foucault would say that the aura of expert knowledge even extends to the way in which I govern my own actions and habits. I am not always being watched and evaluated, but the things I do even in private are patterned by the feeling that somewhere someone *is*. The reporting of expert findings in newspapers, magazines, and other popular media achieves this effect very well. Particularly this is the case in the area of what we physically consume. Our choices about what to purchase, cook, and eat are frequently driven by the concern that we ought to conform to what the experts say about what we ought to eat, or by the feeling that a certain size of body is the healthy norm for a person of my age and gender. An expert dietician and an expert fashionista will probably say very different things about food; but both exert an influence on the non-professional world by means of their expertise.

II QUESTIONING THE EXPERTS?

Monty Python's *The Meaning of Life* opens with a woman giving birth in a hospital. The camera gives us her point of view as her trolley-bed is wheeled into the operating theater and as the two doctors shout commands to one another and the hospital staff. At one point she bravely asks "what can I do, doctor?"—to which the doctors instantly reply "Nothing, dear—you're not qualified!" The point is clear: we aren't supposed to resist, or even to try to help, the expert. We just have to lie back and let them do what they are trained and paid to do. Even something as normal and natural as giving birth is now carried out under the supervision of white-coated experts.

The problem with the cult of expertise is that we have no way really to check the expert's advice. We can get another opinion, but then it is just a case of expert against expert, and we are not necessarily better off. We just have to believe them: which means they have an incredible amount of power over us. I might possibly gain consolation by finding my own area of expertise, so that at least I have something to bring to the social table. But this does not mitigate the feeling that I have that if the expert is wrong, I am liable to suffer for his mistakes—and there's nothing I can do about it.

The case of climate change is a good example. Is it the case that the climate is changing because of human-created environmental damage? Well, many of the experts are agreed that this is the case. Indeed, to be fair, an overwhelming majority of acknowledged experts are saying just this. I might say "science says that anthropogenic climate change is real"; but when I do, I am just saying what the expert scientists are saying this at the moment. I personally have no idea whether or not it is in a direct sense. I am completely unable to evaluate the scientific data for myself—and, if I could, I wouldn't have time. So I am in the hands of the experts, who will inform government policies and whether I should pay a tax on my use of carbon.

This feels like a looser grip on the truth (or not) than we'd like; and it's precisely this looseness that climate change skeptics exploit. But how can we get around it? Now, you could have an attempt by experts to democratize their knowledge so that it becomes the possession of the inexpert. Al Gore's (1948–) lecture-film *An Inconvenient Truth* (2006) was an example of precisely this strategy. Clearly, Gore realized that a blather of scientific jargon wasn't going to win over non-experts at a deep level to the degree that their behaviors were transformed. So he packaged the expert information in a mass medium and used clever diagrams and animations to communicate his message.

But it isn't easy to do successfully. Gore's film was inevitably open to the accusation that he had bent the truth to fit the medium. While he was, according to scientists who reviewed the film, accurate in his main thesis and in many of the details, in some areas he was clearly guilty of rhetorical excess. The connection between hurricanes and climate change, for example, is a contentious matter amongst scientists. Yet the images of the devastating impact of Hurricane Katrina provided an alarming backdrop to Gore's message—one that was unjustified on the basis of the scientific evidence. Or at least: that's what the experts I consulted said . . .

So, the attempt to communicate expert knowledge in a non-expert way does not give a non-expert grounds to challenge the experts. I couldn't justifiably contradict a climate-change scientist on the basis of a viewing of *An Inconvenient Truth*. The film gives me knowledge that is agreed to be largely trustworthy, but watching it does not convey to me the kind of status and authority that we accord an expert.

But clearly, experts are not always right, and need to be challenged at some point. For a start, it is almost in the nature of expert knowledge that it is disputed. Expert disagreement is to be expected, because the level of detail and the sophistication required of expertise, in almost any area, means there is room for differing interpretations. This is more likely to be the case in more speculative fields of knowledge, of course. Expert economists will make widely varying, even contradictory, pronouncements about the future. And clearly they can't all be right, even though they are acknowledged experts in their field. Though they have all the qualifications in the world, they may be exactly *wrong*.

What's more, cognitive neuro-scientific studies have argued that the possession of expert knowledge may in fact make experts more prone to certain sorts of error. Psychologist Itiel E. Dror (1961–) argues that through their long years of training, experts develop certain "cognitive architecture" that enables them to quickly access the kind of knowledge they need. That's what makes them expert. However, Dror writes:

> These information processing mechanisms, the very making of expertise, entail computational trade-offs that sometimes result in paradoxical functional degradation.[2]

That is: all the shortcuts that experts develop in their brain structure may result in a vulnerability to certain kinds of error. Experts rely on quickly surmising the context of information; but these very habits of mind

> restrict flexibility and control, may cause the experts to miss and ignore important information, introduce tunnel vision and bias and can cause other effects that degrade performance. Such phenomena are apparent in a wide range of expert domains, from medical professionals and forensic examiners, to military fighter pilots and financial traders.[3]

Thirdly, experts may be as prone to groupthink as any other group of human beings. They may act in a collective way, such that a powerful set of underlying assumptions is held to be unchallengeable. This may have financial consequences in the area of research grants and publications and so forth—which makes for a powerful pressure on individual experts to

2. Dror, "The Paradox of Human Expertise," 177.
3. Ibid.

conform to the assumptions of the group. Or it could be that a pre-existing ideological commitment leads to a skewing of the evidence away from what is in fact the case. The impact of Marxism on the academic world of Eastern Europe in the middle of the twentieth century is a case in point.

Given the trust we place in expert knowledge, the consequences of expert error are often woeful. Consider the case of Sir Roy Meadow (1933–), the British professor of pediatrics who made his name as an expert in the field of child abuse. His name became associated with "Meadow's Law," which stated that "one sudden infant death is a tragedy, two is suspicious and three is murder, until proved otherwise." Meadow appeared as an expert witness in a number of trials, and his testimony was instrumental in gaining convictions of a number of people who had lost babies to cot death. Among these was Sally Clark, a solicitor who was tried in 1999 for the murder of her two babies Christopher and Harry. Meadow testified that the odds of a family experiencing two cot deaths were 73,000,000 to 1. A far more likely explanation, he claimed, was that Clark had smothered her children while suffering from post-natal depression. This was later shown to be a statistical nonsense. Clark's conviction was eventually overturned on a number of grounds and she was released from prison in 2003; but the damage to her was done, and she died of alcohol poisoning four years later.[4]

The flaws in Meadow's expertise were discovered, but only through the rigorous application of expertise against him. One problem was endemic to the cult of experts: Meadow was an expert in his own field, but ranged into an area—statistics—in which he was clearly only an amateur. Yet because of the aura of expertise, he was believed by intelligent and well-meaning people, from the police to the lawyers and the juries involved, whose job it was to scrutinize the evidence available. A person who knows a lot about one thing may easily convey the impression that he knows a lot about everything, when in fact he does not at all.

But there's no way around this impasse other than the rigorous application of . . . expert knowledge. The Meadow case shows us that expert knowledge has a narrowness which may give it blind spots. Exposure to other fields of expertise can remedy some of the damage an expert error may cause. However, this solution is nothing other than a slow process of checking and rechecking data and of allowing for the public discussion of ideas. The best we can do is to equip ourselves with the kind of healthy reserve that the best experts have towards even their own work: an attitude

54. See Sweeney and Law, "Gene Find Casts Doubt."

that will prepare us for the discovery that what we thought to be the considered consensus of expert opinion may turn out after all to be entirely mistaken. Allowing for this, it seems perfectly appropriate to trust the experts in most cases; indeed, in the case of climate change, it hardly seems legitimate to contradict them. We can do no more that make ourselves aware of the humanness of all knowing. And practice patience.

III CONSPIRACY THEORIES AND CRANKS

We have seen how vulnerable we are to the cult of expertise. Whose interests do experts serve? Are they practicing groupthink, or blinded by their narrowness? Why should I trust them? We don't like the feeling of having to accept received opinion, either.

And expert knowledge has in the past been overturned by outsiders and crackpots—people who weren't considered experts by the experts. Whatever impression they might give, experts are not infallible. There are gaps in all knowledge. There are unexplained phenomena, statistical oddities, theoretical impossibilities, and unexplored fields.

There are three common temptations that flow from the evident limitations of expert knowledge. The first is to foster a stubborn skepticism towards all expert knowledge. This is the temptation of the climate-change denier. Admittedly, the smugness of proponents of climate-change regarding their claims can be galling to the ordinary person. Likewise, it is sometimes easy to associate them with ideological and political interests which may have a distorting effect on their science.[5] It is epistemologically right to hold the claims being made for the science of climate change at arm's length, for, like all human knowledge, there is room for error.

But the persistent skeptic points to the fact that there are holes in the theory in question and to the incompleteness or the complexity of the available knowledge and claims that this means that the whole theory must be bunk. Where there is not 100 percent certainty, there is room for doubt. But that room may be a very small alcove in which you can barely fit a potted plant. Indeed: where there is a claim for 100 percent certainty, we should be skeptical of the maths involved!

---

5. I would hasten to add that criticism of climate change scientists and their claims is also vulnerable to the accusation that it is a merely rhetorical move used to deflect the "inconvenient truths" about our contemporary lifestyles that climate change science exposes.

The second temptation—which is not unrelated—is to cling to conspiracy theories. If expert opinion is slanted in one direction, then the conspiracy theorist claims that the slant is due to some secret agenda or bias. Expert knowledge is extremely difficult to outflank, especially if there is a strong consensus. This leads to the disempowerment of those not in the know. The conspiracy theory is an attempt to subvert the power of expertise by claiming that the pose of "expert" knowledge has been assumed in order to mask the real truth. It may be claimed, for example, that the 9/11 attacks on the World Trade Centre never occurred, and that a conspiracy of government agencies pulled off an extraordinary fraud on the American public in front of the eyes of the world in order to provide a pretext for military action in the Middle East. Or, a young earth creationist may claim that the scientists who claim that the earth is old do so under the influence of a set of ideological assumptions that lead them to bracket out the real evidence—and that the worldwide scientific community, because of its bias towards atheism, places strong pressure on those who disagree. Perhaps this is better described as a "mass delusion" theory, or a "mass ideological bias" theory. Nevertheless, both are attempts to account for the way in which expert knowledge is weighted overwhelmingly against their view.

The fascinating thing about conspiracy theorists is the way in which they mimic the forms of expert knowledge that they are seeking to question. So, we find young earth creation "scientists" parading their PhDs, and 9/11 conspiracy theorists consulting "experts" and providing very detailed accounts of their ideas, complete with apparently plausible statistics and pseudo-scientific information. Conspiracy theorists know that they can seem believable if they present baffling mumbo-jumbo that makes people feel like something truly clever is going on. Thus, conspiracy theorists both play the game of expert knowledge *and* at the same time seek to undermine it. If you've claimed that the whole guild of scientific experts is corrupt or fundamentally self-deceived, then why does having one of their qualifications matter a jot?

The third epistemological temptation that is worth describing is the phenomenon of the "crank." The crank is a person who holds stubbornly to a belief despite the overwhelming consensus of his or her contemporaries. The classic crank will spend years researching a theory that most experts in the field consider to be spurious or nonsense—becoming, in effect an expert in nonsense. Cranks are often oblivious to their misunderstandings of fundamental concepts in their chosen fields, but highly resistant to any attempt to clear these up.

The trouble is, sometimes the cranks are right. Modern-day cranks love to compare themselves to Copernicus (1473–1543) or Galileo (1564–1642) as examples of scientists who were independent spirits in their own times, and were considered cranks by their contemporaries. There are more recent examples, too. One of these is J. Harlen Bretz (1882–1981). In the 1920s, Bretz began to present evidence which challenged the prevailing view of geologists that the Earth's features had been carved out by a gradual process of erosion and rock-forming over a vast span of time. What Bretz argued was that there were some significant events in geological history that could have an impact over a very short time. Volcanic eruptions or meteoric collisions could have dramatic, relatively instant effects on the Earth's geological features. Bretz came to his conclusions after studying the Scablands in Northwest America and determining that only a massive deluge of water could have accomplished the things he observed there.

Now, Bretz did have a PhD in geology; but his original training had been in biology. When he first published his ideas, he was dismissed out of hand by the leaders in the field. Furthermore, when another geologist, Joseph Pardee (1871–1960), decided that Bretz was right, he was put under enormous pressure not to support him publicly. Here was an egregious instance of groupthink at work. At a public forum of the Geological Society in Washington, Bretz was invited to present his theory. But he was opposed by an organized opposition of six expert, Ivy League geologists. It was an ambush, designed to humiliate Bretz and drive him from the field. It wasn't until the 1950s, once the impact of the Ice Age had become more widely understood, that Bretz's views were fully vindicated. When he was finally recognized for his contribution to geology in 1979 when he was ninety-six, he rather ruefully commented: "my enemies are dead, so I have no one to gloat over."[6]

Bretz was a crank who turned out to be right, because sometimes cranks *are* right. The experts sought to bully him and to censor his views. The trouble is that examples like that of Bretz do not give us warrant to believe cranks (and not experts) simply because they, like Bretz, stand against prevailing orthodoxy. The reason Bretz was right was that he studied the evidence more carefully than his opponents. That the crank is sometimes right doesn't mean the crank is always right.

6. MacDougall, *Frozen Earth*, 105.

Expert knowledge is limited; but that limitation is not fatal to the way in which expert knowledge functions in our specialized society. That our knowledge is provisional doesn't mean it isn't knowledge. Indeed, insofar as we are non-experts, we actually have no warrant to decide for the cranks.

However, we do need to recognize that a trust is fundamental to the whole process by which we learn and know things. That is: we need to develop not simply a skill in reasoning but the ability to trust others and to be worthy of the trust of others. In this way we can see that, without faith, reason is dead.

What has this discussion of expert knowledge got to do with believing *in God?* It shows us at least that the process by which we come to have religious faith is not as foreign, or as spooky, as some people make out, since we involve the operation of trust in our everyday acts of knowing all the time. Our need for trust in others suggests that believing in God and believing in other things are not altogether different. What we need to do now is to probe this suspicion.

IV THE GETTING OF WISDOM

I have spoken about the limitations of expert knowledge not in order to prompt a kind of endless suspicion against it but rather so that we recognize it for what it is and what it gives us—and how dependent we are on it, even though it doesn't always deliver the certainty we want. By no means would I like to be heard encouraging an unwarranted faith in cranks and conspiracy theories.

But expert knowledge is limited in a couple of other important ways that we often fail to recognize. Let's return to Dr. Mort's surgery, where we find the good doctor allowing me to consult him about my brain tumor. Only, he's not a "good" doctor. I don't mean that he is a bad *doctor.* No, he is simply bad. Because of some specialized research I have been doing, I instantly recognize him as a wanted man: he was once a torturer for a dictatorial South American regime that has been overturned. How do I feel now about putting my life in his hands? At one level, neither his expertise nor his skill is necessarily compromised by his grim track record. But there's something profoundly disturbing about the thought of allowing such a person access to the status and authority of one of the expert professions.

Why is this so disturbing? Well, an encounter with a former torturer will no doubt be disturbing, but that's not what I had in mind. It's unsettling because there's an underlying cultural assumption that a member of one of the expert professions will be a generally respectable person in possession not only of expert knowledge but also of a number of virtues—honesty, integrity, compassion, not torturing people, and so on. But why should we assume this? We can, granted, assume that the person with his or her name on the metal plate next to the surgery is (or at least, was at one time) in possession of self-discipline and capable of hard work. Yet medical training is not a school for virtue; it is a school for medical knowledge. Perhaps there were a couple of ethics classes along the way, but that's not the same thing as the cultivation of the kind of virtues of which I imagine a medical specialist to be in possession.

This is a problem for two reasons. One the one hand, expert knowledge is, as we have noted, a powerful weapon to wield within a community. It accrues trust. An expert who lacks virtue is a very dangerous individual indeed; and to the degree that any expert lacks virtue, there is a danger of our trust being misplaced or misused. On the other, we often give the expert in one field the right to speak about other fields, assuming that success in one thing is the same as getting life generally right.

That is, we think that experts have *wisdom* when what they really have is *knowledge,* or *skill.* They may of course be very wise, but we don't know that just from recognizing them as experts. We can see it most crassly in the cult of celebrity, which holds up successful musicians, sports stars, and actors as people whose life-skills are worth emulating. At the same time, we gawp at their drug addictions, weight loss/gain issues, and broken relationships. But we also do allow "scientists," for example, to pronounce on all manner of subjects. Richard Dawkins is a classic case: he is undoubtedly expert in his chosen field of evolutionary biology. But he is a rank amateur in the fields of history and philosophy, as has been repeatedly shown by his critics and reviewers. He is certainly not a specialist in geology and in astronomy. Nevertheless, his right to make pronouncements in these fields is simply granted to him because of the aura of his expertise.

It is perfectly reasonable for us to want some integration of knowledge, because we need information and analysis from across different fields if we are going to address some of life's most pressing questions—such as the existence of God and the meaning of right and wrong. A single discipline cannot carry us very far on these questions. The concept of the "university" was originally derived from the view that all knowledge was interlocking and overlapping; and thus it was beneficial to have students and teachers from all fields of knowledge working side by side in a single institution of learning. This ideal has become very much degraded in the present time, with the opening of separate schools for different disciplines and with economic forces ensuring that interdisciplinary work is harder and harder to undertake. There is also a loss of a vision for how the university is indeed united; and instead, we experience the fragmentation of knowledge into disconnected areas.

The integration of the disciplines of knowledge is an ethical and indeed ultimately a theological issue. Expert knowledge gained in a single area without reference to the other disciplines of knowledge is an open door for human pride. It feeds the illusion of a human omniscience. The other disciplines of knowledge can provide a proper balance to the hubris of the expert. And this depends on a kind of faith—a faith which can be understood in a secular way, although it has theological roots. This is a faith that the universe is a meaningful and integrated whole and that we can study it on the presumption that ultimately it makes sense, whether we can see that sense at this point in time or not. The universe's coherence could never be grasped in its entirety, but nevertheless, we proceed on the assumption that it holds together somewhere, somehow. The detective is right (we all agree) to proceed on the basis that there is some explanation for the murder of the person lying in the morgue with a large stab wound apparently made by a bowie knife under his left nipple. That he may never find the perpetrator doesn't mean there wasn't one.

Of course, the theologian at this point wants to say to the atheist or agnostic—"you have a working assumption of the universe's coherence, but no reason to believe it in particular. There's plenty in the universe that is mysterious and confounding: take the baffling business of quantum mechanics, for example. Why should we simply assume that it all makes sense, rather than that simply being a fantasy in which we indulge?" The theologian, on the other hand, has a way of explaining why the mystery of the universe is only mysterious because of the limitations of our finite and terrestrial minds. This is not a proof of the existence of God, of course. But it is a choice for a kind of consistency.

The business of human knowing is also rightly described as an "ethical" concern because human knowledge advances within certain "societies of knowledge." That is, knowing things is a fundamentally and inescapably social activity. The relationships that help us to know things exist as *traditions* (one's forebears in a discipline) and *communities* (one's contemporaries).

Even individual geniuses in the history of human knowledge built on the things that had been bequeathed to them by the generation before; and had to operate in relation to academic guilds and societies and so on. What awareness of your place in a tradition and a community helps you to see is that what human beings know and learn is profoundly linked to where we sit in relation to others. I used the word "ethical" at this point because, wherever human communities are concerned, we are called upon to consider how we treat one another. Even if you are standing on the shoulders of a giant, and thus seeing farther than the giant, you are still dependent on the giant.

Let me take this thread of thought a little further. If we understand the importance of traditions and communities in helping us to know things, we will have to acknowledge how dependent we are not only on their accuracy of mind and commitment to the truth but also that, if there is a malevolent strain lurking within a tradition or a community, that we will be able to recognize it and weed it out. There is implicit in the ideas of tradition and community some vision of what it is to act rightly—an *ethos,* we might say. And this vision is not simply generated from within the tradition or the community. It comes from somewhere outside of them.

V THE WISDOM OF FAITH

Thus far I have been trying to show how, in our dependence on expert knowledge, we of necessity have to engage ourselves in multiple acts of trust every day. As a result, Western culture has a tendency to idolize experts and at times is blind to the mistakes experts make—with terrible consequences. At the same time, there are those who exploit the appearance of expert errors to promote conspiracy theories and crank-ism. This is simply illegitimate. With all the caveats in place, expert knowledge is a great blessing and we are right to trust it with our lives. But we should also be aware that expert knowledge needs to be—indeed, simply *is*—part of a whole enterprise of human understanding. Expert knowledge in a certain field is not the same as knowledge of how to live—and yet, expert knowledge without life-wisdom is extremely volatile. This has drawn us into the consideration of the ethical—and the theological, too.

These observations resonate with what we find in scripture. "Wisdom," *hokmah,* as the Old Testament describes it, certainly makes room for the kind of expert knowledge that comes from disciplined attention to a single area of the world. But it is also integrative: it shows the deep, beautiful coherence of the world as the work of a single creator. And it is practical: it is concerned with how human beings can best live in response to his call. It is no accident that the secret to its discovery, repeated as a constant refrain in the book of Proverbs, is "the fear of the Lord." "The fear of the Lord is the beginning of wisdom" (9:10) is the axiom of axioms, the motto of mottos.

True worship, in other words, is the ground of an integrated, practical, and expert knowledge. The expression "the fear of the Lord" articulates the kind of humility we already sense should be part of the enterprise of seeking to know the world. To fear the Lord, *Yahweh* (the special name of God), the God of Israel, is to revere the one who led Israel out of Egypt with a strong arm and a mighty hand. He is the lawgiver, who makes a covenant with his people and commands them to obey him. That is: fear of the Lord entails recognizing the prospect of giving him account for one's actions. But this is, in turn, based on God's initial movement *towards* human beings in grace and salvation. Yahweh is not simply the judge. He's the savior who judges.

Hence the kind of "fear" that is described in wisdom is not a fear that freezes you to the spot in knee-knocking dread. It is rather a fear that enables—a reverence for one whose character is known rather than a terror at someone who is unpredictable and unknowable. "Fear" has an unpleasant sound in contemporary ears; but the one who fears Yahweh is equipped with the brilliant insight that he or she is not divine. Humility before the creator is the basis for knowing the creation—the supreme virtue of knowledge.

This stance before God is "the *beginning* of wisdom." It is foundational, but it isn't comprehensive. The one who simply "fears the Lord" has more work to do. Faith precedes knowledge—in fact it makes true knowledge possible. It is like a light that shines on the world and makes understanding it real. You need to submit to God to see how all knowledge makes sense. Right regard for God is the proper starting point for wisdom—"the beginning." To get wise, you need to begin with this perspective. It isn't the totality of wisdom. It is the beginning, the springboard from which we are to jump, the platform on which we are to build. And this tells us something crucial—wisdom is not dictated to us. It is there for us to find—in fact it is a human responsibility, as God-fearers, to seek it out.

But the fear of the Lord is also wisdom's goal. It is where wisdom will take us in the end. In Proverbs 2:1–5 we read:

My son, if you accept my words
and store up my commands within you,
turning your ear to wisdom
and applying your heart to understanding—
indeed, if you call out for insight
and cry aloud for understanding,
and if you look for it as for silver
and search for it as for hidden treasure,
then you will understand the fear of the Lord
and find the knowledge of God.

Knowledge, if pursued to its end, will return us to its own foundation. The discovery of the world will not divert us from God, but direct us to him.

Well, it ought to, under "ordinary" conditions. The world as the Book of Proverbs describes it is regular and predictable. Even though there is evil in it, you can see it coming if you are wise to it. But there is another perspective to the world, too. Wisdom is not complete without the much more jaundiced view of the Teacher in the book of Ecclesiastes, and the horrors that Job encounters. These works you could almost term "anti-wisdom"; because they recognize that a common human experience is not that a little bit of canny sense of the everyday world will get you through, but that what the world clearly *ought* to be like is very evidently not what it is like. Under normal conditions, we can see that the life that is truly wise is lengthier, healthier, and happier. But there's not a guarantee that this will be the case. The non-smoker, a wise person if ever there was one, may still get lung cancer. The vegetarian gets a heart attack. The happy family man and devoted husband wakes up to find his wife has left him. A car accident takes the life of the careful driver with her seatbelt on. Absurdity crushes in on normality.

A lot of people think that the Bible gives "answers" to these questions. It does nothing of the kind. It fact, in the book of Job we see the kind of cheap theological answer to the absurdity of life satirized. But the refrain "the fear of the Lord" is not exhausted by these occurrences. It is not overthrown by them. It is a signal that the existence of a Lord of the kind that the narrative of the Bible describes is the ground for substantial hope. This is not a revelation of the answers, but a revelation of the one in whom all answers lie.

That last statement shouldn't sound cheap, as if it is a rabbit pulled from a hat. It isn't, because you still have to sit sometimes like Job in the dust scratching your sores with a piece of pottery. There's no getting around that. That's not what Christian hope offers. It isn't a way around: it is only a way *through*.

Six

Getting the Joke

That night, that year
Of now done darkness I wretch lay wrestling with (my God!) my God.

GERARD MANLEY HOPKINS (1844–89)

I HA!

What does it mean to believe, from where we twenty-first-century people sit? We have so far considered faith in the light of some of the peculiar conditions under which it has to labor in our time: grief and death; the burdened conscience; time; expert knowledge. If there's been a common thread running throughout, it is that, in general, believing as such is more ordinary human behavior than we perhaps think it is.

But what is *Christian* faith like, in itself?

It is like getting a joke.

The American writer Fredrick Buechner (1926–) once said:

81

> Is it possible, I wonder, to say that it is only when you hear the
> Gospel as a wild and marvelous joke that you really hear it at all?[1]

You can certainly hear a joke without "getting" it. Consider how a person operating in a language that is not her native language will take something intended to be a joke quite literally. She may be quite fluent in the second language; but getting its jokes is usually the last thing to fall into place. "Getting it" involves an almost intuitive grasping of the connections in what is being said. That is why humor is central to the formation of group identity: a shared joke is almost like a private language. British comedian Milton Jones (1964–) has written, "My faith is like a joke—some people get it and some people don't, and some people pretend they get it, and some people pretend they don't."[2]

And what makes a joke funny is the way in which several apparently absurd or bewildering items will line up all at once and suddenly make sense. A joke—especially in the form of a pun—is a sudden shock of meaning. Two unlikely ideas suddenly make a peculiar sense that was unforeseen by the listener; but once they do, nothing is quite the same again. As Walter Redfern (1936–) writes in his (dead-pan serious) book *Puns*: "Laughter, and fresh ways of looking, alike depend often on the clash or merger between two universes . . . By such rearrangements, meaning is inflicted."[3] Stagger me (as we say in Australia): a new perspective has come into view! It's the squirt in the eye from the flower you thought was a flower but which turned out to be water-squirter disguised as a flower.

The great Swiss theologian Karl Barth (1886–1968) is alleged to have said "Laughter is close to the grace of God."[4] It is the element of surprise that makes laughter like grace: it is unnecessary, so non-karmic. It "travels outside karma," as U2 put it. God's grace, this profoundly divine quality of free generosity, is not the way the world appears to work. We are used to the remorseless grinding of the fortune's wheel; we assume that for every action there is an equal and opposite reaction. Divine grace seems to subvert the apparently "natural" order of things, and make possible a new alignment of reality. You cannot trace it through cause-and-effect. It is incalculable.

---

1. Buechner, *Telling the Truth*, 68.

2. Jones, *10 Second Sermons*, Kindle edition.

3. Redfern, *Puns*, 27–28.

4. I have been unable to find a direct source for this quote from Barth.

You can't see this if you understand "God" as simply proposition in a philosophical syllogism. That pseudo-deity is boringly predictable and will act (or not) only within the prism of his definition.

But who is *this* God, whose grace is so close to laughter? It is the storyline of Bible that discloses him: the story of his dealings with humanity which reaches its climax in the appearance of Jesus Christ, which is more than a little surprising. In other words: this is the God who is the one who sent Jesus and who, after he was killed, raised him from the dead. That is who he is—the one who did those unexpected things.

My thesis is this: however strange it sounds, the gospel of the God of Jesus is comic. What do I mean exactly? I use the word "gospel" for two reasons. First, it is "gospel" because it indicates that we are talking about *news*—about a series of events that have occurred and are now conveyed as a message, a story. Second, it is "gospel" because a gospel demands a response. It is conveyed to an audience, who either recognizes it as good news, or rejects it as offensive, foolish, or irrelevant. They may even stone the messenger. People either get it, or they don't, in other words.[5] Like a joke.

The gospel is comic because it involves the surprising and ironic inversion of the way we expect things to be; and it is comic because it narrates a story in which order is brought from chaos, good through bad, something from nothing. Simply put: despite everything, *it ends well.*

The Christian gospel is surprising. It isn't what you'd expect, not at all. And, unsurprisingly, some people just don't get it. It's why the disciples are portrayed—and, more surprisingly, allowed themselves to be portrayed—as such dolts, as they struggled with "getting" Jesus in the Gospels. "You are the Christ!" says Peter; and then he rebukes Jesus when he explains how the Son of Man is going to be betrayed and suffer. At this point Jesus calls him satanic for his insistence that the suffering of the cross had no place in the Messiah's story.

But we have come at our observation—"that the gospel is surprising and unexpected"—from the point of view of the response that it gets. The gospel surprises people, fair enough: but is there something in it that is inherently a shock? The life and teaching of Jesus demonstrated the surprise and irony at the heart of God's work in the world. His life was full of

---

5. I don't mean by this that, if you don't seem to "get it" at once, then it is simply inaccessible. That's not true of humor, anymore than it is of Christian faith. It presents itself as a tease; as a thread to be pulled; as an invitation to go further in.

incongruities from the start. One of the scenes in which this is most apparent is when the angel Gabriel visits the Virgin Mary to announce to her own pregnancy. Her naïve-but-knowing asking of the obvious question—"How can this be, since I am a virgin?"—highlights the surprise that God would work in this fleshly way. The song she sings shows that she now gets the joke:

> My soul praises the Lord and my spirit rejoices in God my Saviour,
> for he has remembered the humble state of his servant.
> From now on all generations will call me blessed . . .
> He has brought down rulers from their thrones
> but has lifted up the humble.
> He has filled the hungry with good things
> but has sent the rich away empty. (Luke 1:46a–53)

It's a song whose theme is inversions. The work of God reverses the order of human expectations. Mary herself has no heroism, no special piety that marks her out for this role. Those traditions that have focused on her alleged purity or virtue somehow miss the point. Her virginity is not significant because that is a sign of her heroic faith and extraordinary uprightness of life. It is rather a mark of the astonishment of what is about to happen to her.

That God would become human is completely surprising. It would make more sense for him to steer clear, and not sully himself with the too, too sullied flesh, with its bacterial bowels and its damp orifices, with its liquids, solids, and gases. Instead, a king is born in poverty, a child gets Herod in a state that he will lose his state; and the Son of Man came not to be served but to serve. The apostle Paul waxes lyrical about it, saying that Jesus was the one who "did not consider equality with God something to be grasped but emptied himself taking the form of a servant" (Phil 2:6–7). Christ's own being—"the form of a servant"—was an embodiment of his teaching. He puts himself at our disposal; and was disposed.

In Jesus's teaching we can see the pattern of reversals in the structure of his message even in the form he uses. In the Sermon on the Mount, he proclaims the meek as inheritors of the earth—they are called "blessed," when plainly they aren't. But because of the gospel, though they are wretched and outcast, they are free to be joyously happy now because of the coming of the kingdom. And, conversely: "woe to you who laugh now, for you will mourn and weep."

Jesus delighted in upside down-ness—"first last, last first," "exalted humbled, humbled exalted"—and in hyperbole: "if your hand causes you to sin, cut it off." There is fear and warning in these if you don't get it; but a promise of joy to those who are in it. The rich young ruler who came to Jesus asking "who can be saved?" is a case in point—he definitely didn't get it, feeling justified in his own eyes and clinging for life to his lifestyle. Jesus's suggestion to him is preposterous—that he "sell all he has and come follow me"—but we are dealing with the God of the impossible, who mightn't exactly pull rabbits out of hats but does fit camels through the eyes of needles.

The parables of Jesus of course require you to "get" them—to have ears to hear, as the model parable, the parable of the sower, shows. In the parable that we call the Good Samaritan the ideas of "Good" and "Samaritan" are bizarrely yoked together. Who'd've thought it—the Samaritans being an ethnically dubious group of ne'er do wells? The tale of the Great Banquet has us laughing at the pathetic excuses of the invited guests, and then at the thought of the "the blind, the halt and the lame" people being welcomed in. One of my favorites is the Pharisee and the Tax Collector, where the good guy gets it wrong in his pomposity, and the filthy sinner crawling in on his hands and knees gets it exactly right. This parable is outrageous, and almost no one gets it; it reverses entirely our expectation of how things should work out.

The miracles of Jesus were in fact stage-managed acts of communication. The evangelist John makes the point by calling them "signs," not miracles. The turning of water into wine is a delightful crowd pleaser, with the punch line: "the best has been left till now." Jesus reversed the usual pattern of serving wine as a graphic illustration of the happy surprise of his own mission on earth. Of course the cross was the greatest reversal of Jesus's life—the glory of the king, the enthronement of the messiah, the great moment of his power—turned out to be his passion. There he hung, labeled "the king of the Jews," with one on his right and one of his left. The sarcastic mockery of the soldiers who put a crown of thorns on his head and gave him a purple, royal robe is viewed through the lens of a further level of irony. They were, unbeknownst to themselves, exactly right. Surprise, surprise.

In the writings of Paul, who himself met a great reversal on the road to Damascus, we see the working out in a life of a great experience of surprising turnabout. When he talks about the cross this becomes most evident. It is the unlikely event *par excellence*—the revelation of the power of God from heaven itself, the moment at which God's impossible love for even his enemies is demonstrated conclusively at the instant when he both satisfied his justice and justified the guilty.

To get yourself crucified was a piece of rank idiocy. From a human perspective it was a mad strategy—if you could call it a "strategy" at all, that is. This is Paul's insight in the first of his letters to the church in Corinth. Written in the midst of a religious power struggle complete with church politics, Paul explains the perverse alternative of a crucified king. It is "foolishness to those who are perishing but to us who are being saved it is the power of God." Just as some didn't "get" Jesus and so crucified him, so the clever and the religious don't get the pathetic, humiliating, shameful cross. It makes only a funny kind of sense; but if you are being saved by it, it is fantastic. God "chose the foolish things of the world to shame the wise; the weak things to shame the strong." To show that he is not impressed by our posturing—even and especially our religious posturing—God chose the most unlikely things as his way to work, including Paul's own weakness and fear.

The joke is on the strong: the weak things, the lowly things are triumphant. As Archbishop Desmond Tutu (1931–) once said:

> We may be surprised at the people we find in heaven. God has a soft spot for sinners. His standards are quite low.[6]

"Getting it" is what true spirituality looks like. It is the Spirit who enables people to get it. As Paul says: "The person without the Spirit does not accept the things that come from the Spirit of God but considers them foolishness, and cannot understand them because they are discerned only through the Spirit" (1 Cor 2:14). The very weakness and unlikeliness of the cross is the reason it is a real act of God. But only the Spirit opens your eyes to see it.

The gospel is comic in the sense that it involves inversions and surprises, and responding to it involves a changed perspective. But it is also comic in that it brings good out of, and through, evil. As a narrative it shares a basic outline with comedy in that through the process of resolving complications what results is even better than that with which you started. This is the delightful outworking of God's sovereignty over human affairs;

6. Tutu, "Desmond Tutu Peace Foundation."

and it makes the world seem very different. As the American ethicist Stanley Hauerwas (1940–) puts it:

> To learn to see the world and ourselves through the eyes of the gospel makes the world profoundly comic. Put differently, if you are a Christian, you have nothing to lose, so you might as well tell the truth. Such a truth often surprises and delights us.[7]

The gospel is not, however a comedy in the style of a farce. It isn't all banana peels and custard pies and pokes in the eye. It is comedy that absorbs tragedy: It doesn't ignore it, it overcomes it. It is a surprise that turns the tragic inevitability of the human cycles of sin and self-destruction on its head. Forgiveness—needed for reconciliation—is a comic ending. Theologian Roy Eckhardt (1918–1998) says that humor and forgiveness have a reciprocal relationship:

> Forgiveness enters the dialectic of humor and faith, pointing to the beginnings of reconciliation among all parties. For in the depths of authentic humor, everyone stands forgiven. That's what humor comes down to really: forgiveness.[8]

The resurrection of course is the key moment, the punch line of the gospel comedy. Yes: the best *had* been left till the end. Without it, we would have merely another tragedy with its salutary and gloomy lesson about human nature: like the shooting of Martin Luther King Jr. (1929–68) or Gandhi (1889–1948). The death of Jesus Christ is not, however, merely a tale of warning about what human beings will do to our best individuals; the passion makes no proper sense without the resurrection, which reveals that this was not an merely the termination of an exemplary individual, but the execution of the Son of God, which is ultimately like trying to blow out one of those trick candles: the flame disappears for a moment, but then flashes back into life.

The resurrection was a great surprise even to Jesus's followers. They clearly hadn't expected it even though they remembered Jesus teaching about it. I think this is often forgotten by modern readers: in our prejudice against ancient peoples we assume they saw the miraculous around them everywhere. They expected him to rise, just like a soufflé you put in the oven predictably rises. So, they read their expectations into what actually happened. But in the New Testament the disciples' shock at the resurrection

7. Hauerwas, *Hannah's Child*, 133.

8. Eckhardt, "Divine Incongruity," 399.

is palpable in the recorded accounts.[9] It is an inherently unlikely conclusion to the story and one which is communicated with gentle raillery against the dim-witted disciples. As Paul explains it:

> [Abraham] is our father in the sight of God, in whom he be-
> lieved—the God who gives life to the dead and calls into being
> things that were not. (Rom. 4:17)

God's first joke was to bring a baby out of the aged womb and flaccid loins of Abraham and Sarah (without Viagra), the one called Isaac, or "he laughs." The second was to take a slave people and make them a great nation of people in a fertile land by defeating the greatest military power on the earth, the Egyptians, at the non-battle of the Red Sea. His third was to bring a baby out of a virgin's womb. His fourth was to bring Jesus out of the darkened tomb. This is the God who brings "is" out of "is not." But the comedy is still in motion: there is still, of course, as we experience, an unfulfilled dimension of the gospel. Human beings continue to labor and suffer and to exist under the shadows of futility and death. But the colossal surprise of the resurrection is our promissory note that history will have a comic and not a tragic ending. It results in hope—a reason to smile through our tears, without gritted teeth.

So—what does getting the joke look like? First of all, it results in an upside down life: conversion, as Christians have described it. The Jesus who asks his disciples to forsake possessions and family, who says "let the dead bury their own dead" demands a self-reversal: a taking up of one's own cross and following him in denial of the rights and desires of the self. It means "praying"—which, if you don't "get it," is a complete waste of time.

The history of the world is not an absurdist drama. It isn't a tragedy. It isn't an endless cycle where we are, *Groundhog Day*-like, doomed to repeat all our mistakes. The gospel tells us that history is comic, under the sovereignty of God. Believers live with this idea, as if the ending is going to be a happy one, despite the mess of the present. This is not Stoic resignation, of which the modern version is Monty Python's "always look on the bright

---

9. The resurrection of Jesus is prophesied in the Old Testament, but not in such a way as you'd've expected it. Amongst the Jews of the first century, there was a great deal of disagreement about the significance and nature of the life to come. But almost no one was predicting what the New Testament claims happened. This matters because the resurrection is expected enough to make sense in the light of the Old Testament, but not to the degree that the disciples could have simply concocted it from the ancient texts and—*voila!*—a risen Messiah.

side of life" because you really have nothing to expect but the unexpected. That is simply a technique with which we are supposed to get by, forcing smiles onto our faces in the morning in the hope that a practiced positive outlook will lead to a deep joy and something to hope in.

Second, this getting of the joke results in the call to live foolish lives—to be "fools for Christ." That is: the life of Christian faith runs the risk of the ridicule of others. Paul the apostle of course knew this better than anyone. At the end of the letter we call 2 Corinthians, out of sheer frustration and deep hurt, he speaks almost perversely of his humiliations as a badge of honor. How can this make sense? In the light of the cross of Jesus Christ as the pattern of God's rule over his world, it does make sense. If Christ the ruler was the subject of rejection and humiliation, then it is possible that rejection and humiliation are the signs of belonging to him.

The atheist philosopher Friedrich Nietzsche (1844–1900), he of drooping moustache and long walks in the Swiss Alps, could see this fool- ishness in Christianity; and he deplored it. He once wrote

> Christianity has taken the side of everything weak, base, ill-con-
> stituted, it has made an ideal out of opposition to the preservative
> instincts of strong life.[10]

Christianity contains within it a hope that makes suffering the contempt (and worse) of Nietzsche and his descendants possible for those who hold it.

II **IMPOSSIBLE**

I don't want to conceal anything here. Faith is not the property of heroes and saints, but belongs to the broken and confused. The singer Johnny Cash (1932–2003), for example, might well be one of the "greatest" men of faith of the twentieth century. Yet he was an alcoholic and drug user, and a womanizing divorcee. His amphetamine addiction continued on and off for most of his life, even after he rediscovered his Christian faith in 1968. This was not an uncomplicated man; but he was a man of faith nonetheless. Faith did not make life for Johnny Cash particularly easy. It may have been his redemption, but it was not a final resolution. It did not untangle the web of his life.

---

10. Nietzsche, *The Anti-Christ*, 129.

And that is partly because Christian faith does ask of believers to believe more than the things they see around them in the ordinary world of everyday experience. It does ask of them to believe in the impossible—or at least to think of "possible" in a different way.

Once again we find that the Bible has got to this point before us. The great narratives of the patriarchs in the book of Genesis are, as you might think, case studies of faith in the God of the Bible. But to say that is to make it sound as if what we are going to encounter on a reading of those stories is something like a sweet and pious family story, with all the aesthetic and human richness of cheap religious art.

But these stories are not like that at all. The soap opera of the first four generations of Abrahamsons—of Abraham, his son Isaac, and his son Jacob and his sons—is a twisting tale of selfish desperation, sexual misconduct, and bad parenting. The characters of this particular family are full of humanizing foibles. Even the great patriarch and exemplar of faith himself, Abraham, is as deeply flawed as someone like Johnny Cash.

Their story begins with the voice of God making promises. Seemingly out of the blue, Abraham hears that he is promised a great family, a great land and a great blessing. But even a decade after the promises have come, we find that Abram and Sarai (as their names were then) are still childless. And the strain is starting to tell:

> Now Sarai, Abram's wife, had borne him no children. But she had an Egyptian maidservant named Hagar; so she said to Abram, "The LORD has kept me from having children. Go, sleep with my maidservant; perhaps I can build a family through her."
> Abram agreed to what Sarai said. (Gen 16:1–2)

Childlessness is of itself heartbreaking enough. But in these circumstances the disappointment and frustration must have been acute. Why? At seventy-five years old, Abram was not interested in moving to a retirement resort and playing a few rounds of golf in comfortable slacks. He had sold up and moved everything had to a hostile territory—from his home in Ur, to land of Canaan.

It was all on the basis of the word of God that came to him those years ago. How this voice of God came to him, we are not told; only that he heard it, and responded by believing it. Now ten years on, he has very little to show for his investment.

But during those ten years, though Abram had shown faith in moving from his home in Ur, he had also shown a tendency to want to take matters into his own hands. The storyteller has us find him engaging in an act of self-protection, as down in Egypt he deceives Pharaoh about the true identity of his wife. Here is one of the themes that will re-appear in the biblical story: people believe in the promises of God but want to take them on their terms. They are frustrated with the speed at which God is *not acting*.

In one episode, Abram even engages in a round of parleying with the Lord in which he demands from him more assurance that the promises are in earnest. Even as he accepts God's word—and we read the words "he believed God, and it was credited to him as righteousness"—Abram turns around and demands from God more concrete evidence: "O Sovereign Lord, how can I know that I will gain possession of it?" Right in the middle of the story of the great ideal of biblical faith we find him unimpressed and a bit unconvinced, quibbling with God himself.

Weren't the words of God himself enough for Abram?

Well, no. We discover that it has now been ten years since the move to Canaan, and for any amount of divine speech there is still no baby. And so Sarai comes up with a plan.

It is, I think, too easy for us to write Abram and Sarai off as silly and faithless. We forget what exactly is being asked of them at this point. The promise was deeply personal, because it involved the human bodies of this aged couple. This was a matter of the nitty-gritty of human reproduction. And they must have known, as they saw their bodies fade, and weaken and slide towards death, that the likelihood of any child arriving in the course of nature was now extremely remote.

And what did they have to show for that decade of waiting? They had God's firm promise and commitment. But what was that worth? Was this promise empty? Anyone can make promises and seal oaths. Was it in fact the case—and it must have crossed at least Sarai's mind—that Abram had simply been deluded when he heard the voice of the Lord? And when she thought about the small print of the contract, Sarai could remember that it had specified that the heir to be expected was to be "a son coming from your own body"—that is, from Abram's. No mention had been made of her as a necessary sharer in the promise. And so, her plan seems reasonable enough. Indeed, as she says "The Lord has kept me from having children." If she has no children as yet, is it not that the sovereign Lord has not merely a bit slow about delivering on his promises, but is actually himself keeping her from having children? Is there not the feeling that God is being somewhat perverse in this plan?

As I said, it is too easy for us to stand over this pair of wrinkled doubters and to approach them from the high moral ground. But I think the text itself doesn't want us to be such unsympathetic readers. Scripture refuses to let us have a cheap shot at Abraham and Sarah. What God promises them is, on any reasonable account, unlikely.

There is more that a twenty-first-century person might have in common with this couple than perhaps we realize. Their doubting is characterized by impatience at God's timing on the one hand and bewilderment as to his methods on the other hand. It is not doubt as to God's existence, nor even doubt as to the goodness of his final plan for things, but doubt as to his chosen methods. The sheer humanness of the divine plan appears to be its biggest weakness. I do know the weakness of human flesh—particularly my own, though I am pretty sure of the grubbiness and weakness of other human flesh as well.

What can God mean by making such fallible and broken vessels the channels through which his plan for redemption comes to the world? It seems perfectly plausible for God to be a transcendent and independent being who is mighty to act and whose word becomes reality even as he says it. But when he gets entangled in human affairs and even binds himself to the performance of human bodies—even rather embarrassingly, in the bedroom—then it is that the realist and the pragmatist in me says, "couldn't he do it better?" "How can this be, since I am a virgin?" "How can this be, since I am well advanced in years?" It's as if his sovereign power is a good theory, but perhaps only that.

This is the strange nature of this kind of wrestle to believe—it is a doubt that actually begins with doubt of ourselves as fallen creatures and weak bodies, and grows into a doubt against the God who would interact with such creatures as we are. Our doubt of ourselves as the possible instruments of God's work in the world leads inexorably to doubt of God himself.

It is not as if this doubt of God is unreasonable or idolatrous, as other forms of doubt may be. This kind of doubt is merely a preference for the possible over the impossible, for the likely over the unlikely.

But the temptation that comes to the characters in the story is to try to secure God's promises for him—to speed up the divine plan somewhat. That's what Sarai tries to do of course by presenting the Egyptian Hagar to Abraham as his bedmate. She exchanges the impossible for the possible. At least Hagar is still ovulating, after all. Sarai gives here to Abram as a wife, not merely as concubine—there seems to be no suggestion that some kind of lustful desire in the eighty-five-year-old Abram is being quenched in the curious arrangement. But even so, the methods are questionable. This couple has altered its marriage arrangements before, and it hasn't been exactly honorable.

And sure enough, Hagar becomes pregnant. Is this finally a tangible result that goes beyond a mere word from God? Has Sarai's scheme been a success?

But we see almost immediately that the outcome is miserable for all three adults. Hagar's scorn of her mistress is met by Sarai's mistreatment and Abram's apathy. Though Hagar had been given to Abraham as a wife, she never stopped being a servant. Had Sarai realized the impropriety of her actions and regretted them, that she so resented Hagar even while she was carrying the precious baby?

The irony of Sarai's story is of course that though Hagar's baby is not the baby of the promise to Abram, her baby becomes the recipient of his own promise. God does not allow Hagar to become the hapless victim of the schemes of Sarai. She is met by the angel of God in the wilderness and hears from him a promise that is strikingly similar to the promise Sarai hoped her offspring would receive: "I will so increase your descendants that they will be too numerous to count."

The baby Ishmael, who looks like he is a jigsaw piece from another puzzle that just won't fit in easily anywhere, is in fact the vehicle for God's work, but in a new way. God will not be trapped by the letter of his promises, it turns out. His arm cannot be so easily twisted.

And this appears to be what we are supposed to see: we cannot create the conditions under which God will act. He is not like the ancient deity Baal, whose prophets thought they needed to cajole him into action by dancing and cutting themselves. God is not a latent power that we can use like a spell. And yet that does not make him weak, or untrue to his own word. It is just that his word is not beholden to our word. We should be less surprised that God is so surprising. And perhaps this is the path out of our doubt about his readiness to act and about his curious methods: would a God we could so easily predict be God? The gospel of Jesus Christ just does not conform to human expectations about how divinity should act.

It turned out that for Abram and Sarai, God was waiting until the most impossible moment before he would deliver on his promise. Both Abraham and Sarah in turn would laugh when they heard this promise again, knowing how old they were. It had got the point of comedy as far as they were concerned.

But the joke was on them. When the baby was born, he was given the name Isaac, which means "he laughs," because, as Sarah would say "God has brought me laughter, and everyone who hears about this will laugh with me." That wasn't to be scoffed at.

Like Mary's story, the story of Abram illustrates for us that faith is not heroic. This is great news for doubters. It might seem strange that the New Testament presents doubting Abraham as a model of faith. His faith is offered as the great outflanking maneuver in the historic pattern of God's justification of his people—he believed, and his faith was credited to him as righteousness. The author the letter to the Hebrews has him listed in the roll call of the faithful forerunners of those who now believe.

But in being an example of faith, Abraham is not a *hero* of faith. Faith is not some virtue like courage that deserves credit by being righteousness. Biblical faith is simply a hearing of the word of God as the word of God. It is not an act that deserves any applause. Now, as we have seen, this word of God is always spoken to us in the midst of a life in which it is contested and disputed, and even flatly denied. It is a word about ninety-year-old women having babies, or bedraggled slaves becoming great nations, or about the dead coming back to life. As a word about the future, as a promise, it never comes to us as a completely fulfilled word. There is always a gap. And so we should not be shocked or dismayed when our questions start to fill that gap: how is God going to bring his word to pass? What is God's plan in this bleak circumstance? What proof can I have of God's commitment to his promises? This side of the end of all things, Christian faith will always be attended by these questions. And we find these questions in the Bible itself.

The wrestle to believe is, in a strange way, part of believing itself. Abraham's crafty grandson Jacob, encountering a stranger by the river Jabbok, wrestled him till dawn and wouldn't let him go. He refused to yield unless the stranger blessed him. The stranger said to him:

> Your name will no longer be Jacob [which means "he grasps"], but Israel, because you have struggled with God and with humans and have overcome. (Gen 32:28)

This new name, which became the name of the people of God, means "he struggles with God." I have always found this extraordinary: the people to whom God moves in loving-kindness and to whom he makes promises are named for their wrestle with him. Faith in this God, that is to say, is not a bland suburban matter, like cul-de-sacs and pay TV. It is wrestled out of the things that seem to contradict it.

So why believe? In his shambolic way, against all hope, Abraham believed, though the evidence of his body "as good as dead" contradicted the promise he heard. Why?

Because the character of God has its own inner logic. The word of God rings true to who God is as he reveals himself to us in what the theologians like to call the "history of salvation." It is the evidence of what God actually does that compels us to believe. The truth that we receive when we believe is not deducible in the ordinary sense, or calculable, or even possible as we recognize it. It isn't something that can be abstracted from the particulars—as if there can be a theoretical, as-it-were "faith." It does not apparently follow "natural" laws. But it is consistent with the miracle that there is something rather than nothing. Abraham was "fully persuaded that God had power to do what he had promised." Can he bring about righteousness and justice on the earth? Yes. Will he? He promises to, and he is true to his word.

There was another woman for whom, it is recorded, pregnancy was an impossibility. Not this time because of old age or infertility, but because of her virginity. When the angel's word came to her, she rightly asked "how can this be, since I am a virgin?"

The angel's reply contained the single truth about God that we need to cling to in the face or our own sinfulness and death, and in the face of the impossibility that these can be overcome by any strategy we can devise: *Nothing is impossible with God.*

III **BELIEVING: UNTIDY, BUT POSSIBLE**

I wasn't ever expecting a reader of this book to put it down feeling as if all the difficulties there are with believing in the Christian God have been tidied up in a neat package. This wasn't ever going to be one of those books with handy bullet points at the end of each chapter.

But in part, that's the nature of Christian faith. Paul once talked about seeing "through a glass dimly": you can see the outlines, and the shapes make sense, but the full clarity of vision isn't yet there. The business of believing takes place in the midst of the mess, not aside from it.

You can't be OCD about these things; that's the not the nature of faith, nor of the world we inhabit. In talking to people who have given up their

Christian faith, or who have wrestled with their doubts to the edge of belief, I sometimes find them longing for all uncertainty to disappear. It doesn't. If it did, then we might reasonably suspect ourselves of suffering under a grand delusion, in fact.

This book has, I suppose, been odd in that it has been focused on the activity of believing rather than on the thing that is to be believed. Of course I think that this has been worthwhile, just as a book about looking at art may focus on the activity of looking rather than at the art itself. But it is certainly incomplete without thinking about the actual works of art.

Just so, Christian faith is nothing much at all without its object—namely, Jesus Christ. And that Jesus is what Christian faith is about says a lot about that faith. For one thing, it sits in the mess. Jesus is not an abstract principle, or a deity for whom arguments can be adduced. He is, quite simply and straightforwardly, a man who lived among other people, in a certain time and place. He said and did things; these were remembered and recorded. He met people, and there were those who were able to call him their friend.

It's unremarkable from one angle. But this life in far off, long ago Palestine was, within the ordinary, extraordinary. I find that I cannot read the life of this man as merely an observer or a critic. The life of this man rather, I find, *reads me*. It is a judgement against me. When I look at this life, I see what it means to love my neighbor as myself. I read of a man so absorbed in the business of serving the other's good, that he is self-forgetful to the point of death. Laid against his life, my own is petty and self-serving, and miles from the purpose for which it seems to have been given to me. When I read about him, I no longer believe in myself.

But when I read about him, I find that it *is* possible to believe. What else can I do but cling to this story—to have it inhabit me and own me, to live as if this story were mine?

What you do with this now is really up to you.

A Note of Thanks

Giving thanks is one of those acts which the disappearance of the divine has made more difficult. If you live in a graceless, remorseless cosmos, then giving thanks is really just a form of payment. But I don't believe that. I think we learn true gratitude from the realization that we are utterly dependent on God for even life itself. Thanks to others begins with thanks to him.

This book has been coaxed into existence over a number of years of thinking, reading, and most of all talking. I have never had a thought I didn't say first, and to those who have borne with my loquaciousness over Campos coffee, while running, while taking breaks, while they were trying to work, on Facebook and elsewhere, I say a humble and hearty thanks. Conversations with Chris Spark and Andrew Errington started me off, years back it seems now.

I was able to preach three sermons on the subject of "The Doubting Christian" at my parish church, All Saints' Petersham. Some of that material has ended up in this book, but the responses and feedback of the congregation have changed it immeasurably for the better. Thanks to the rector, Reverend Antony Barraclough, for giving me his pulpit for three weeks.

Also, thanks to Dr. Andrew Cameron and Rebecca Belzer for the chance to air some of the material at the Centre for Christian Living, Moore College. The fifty or so people who came and responded I cannot list by name, but—thanks to you all. A version of chapter 2 appeared in *Quadrant* magazine, for which thanks are due to the editor, Dr. Keith Windschuttle. I had some interesting correspondence as a result of that publication, which stimulated further thought.

Rory Shiner and Nick Moll read the manuscript and offered the kind of searching comments that every author needs. Zac Miles was a diligent and insightful research assistant, chasing references down rabbit holes in the heat of a Sydney December when he could have been at the beach.

I am never more aware of the sweetness of the gift of life than when I am with Catherine and our four children, Simon, Sacha, Matilda, and Freya.

Bibliography

Adams, Scott. "Talent or Handicap." *The Scott Adams Blog,* April 2, 2012. Accessed November 30, 2012. http://dilbert.com/blog/entry/talent_or_handicap/.

Bayer, Oswald. *Martin Luther's Theology: A Contemporary Interpretation.* Translated by Thomas H. Trapp. Grand Rapids: Eerdmans, 2008.

Blasko, Sarah. "Asking Sarah Blasko." *Faster Louder,* January 30, 2005. Accessed November 30, 2012. http://www.fasterlouder.com.au/features/1626/Asking-Sarah-Blasko.

Buechner, Frederick. *Telling the Truth: The Gospel as Tragedy, Comedy, and Fairy Tale.* New York: HarperCollins, 1977.

Cicero. *De Natura Deorum.* Cambridge: Cambridge University Press, 2003.

Csíkszentmihályi, Mihály. *Flow: The Psychology of Optimal Experience.* New York: Harper and Row, 1990.

de Botton, Alain, and Brian Rosner. "Interview with Alain de Botton." Centre for Public Christianity, May 11, 2012. Accessed November 30, 2012. http://publicchristianity.org/library/interview-with-alain-de-botton.

de Botton, Alain. *Religion for Atheists: A Non-believer's Guide to the Uses of Religion.* New York: Pantheon, 2012.

Dostoevsky, Fyodor. *The Brothers Karamazov.* Translated by Richard Pevear and Larissa Volokhonsky. New York: Farrar, Straus and Giroux, 2002.

Dror, Itiel E. "The Paradox of Human Expertise: Why Experts Get It Wrong." In *The Paradoxical Brain,* edited by Narinder Kapur, 177–88. Cambridge: Cambridge University Press, 2011.

Eckhardt, A. Roy. "Divine Incongruity: Comedy and Tragedy in a Post-Holocaust World." *Theology Today* 48L4 (January 1992) 399–412.

Eliot, Thomas Sterns. *Essays Ancient and Modern.* London: Faber and Faber, 1936.

Erikson, Erik H. *Young Man Luther: A Study in Psychoanalysis and History.* New York: Norton, 1962.

Foucault, Michel. *Discipline and Punish: The Birth of the Prison.* Translated by Alan Sheridan. New York: Random House, 1995.

Freud, Sigmund. *The Future of an Illusion.* New York: Classic House, 2009.

Garner, Helen. *The Spare Room.* Melbourne: Text, 2008.

———. *True Stories.* Melbourne: Text, 1996.

Gross, Dick. "Apostates for Evensong." *The Age,* September 5, 2011. Accessed November 30, 2012. http://www.theage.com.au/opinion/blogs/godless-gross/apostates-for-evensong-20110902-1jpix.html.

Harris, Sam. *Free Will*. New York: Free Press, 2012.

Harrison, Peter. "Christianity and the Rise of Western Science." *ABC Religion and Ethics*, May 8, 2012. Accessed November 30, 2012. http://www.abc.net.au/religion/articles/2012/05/08/3498202.htm.

Hauerwas, Stanley. *Hannah's Child: A Theologian's Memoir*. Grand Rapids: Eerdmans, 2010.

James, William. *The Varieties of Religious Experience: A Study in Human Nature*. Rockville, MD: Arc Manor, 2008.

Jones, Milton. *10 Second Sermons: . . . and Even Quicker Illustrations*. London: Darton, Longman and Todd, 2011, Kindle edition.

Kelly, Kevin. *What Technology Wants*. New York: Viking, 2010.

Larkin, Philip. *Collected Poems*. New York: Farrar, Straus and Giroux, 2001. Online: *Poetry Foundation*. Accessed December 5, 2012. http://www.poetryfoundation.org/poem/178046.

Luther, Martin. *Luther's Works*. Vol. 29. Edited by Jaroslav Pelikan. St. Louis: Concordia, 1955–1986.

———. "On the Bondage of the Will." In *Luther and Erasmus: Free Will and Salvation*, edited by E. Gordon Rupp and Philip S. Watson, 101–334. Philadelphia: Westminster, 1969.

MacDougall, Douglas. *Frozen Earth: The Once and Future Story of the Ice Ages*. Berkeley: University of California Press, 2013.

Malouf, David. "The Happy Life: The Search for Contentment in the Modern World." *Quarterly Essay* 41 (2011) 1–56.

Marvell, Andrew. "To His Coy Mistress." In *The Oxford Book of English Verse*, edited by C. Ricks, 186–87. Oxford: Oxford University Press, 1999.

Moltmann, Jürgen. *The Way of Jesus Christ: Christology in Messianic Dimensions*. Translated by Margaret Kohl. London: SCM, 1990.

Nietzsche, Friedrich. *The Anti-Christ*. Translated by R. J. Hollingdale. Harmondsworth: Penguin, 1990.

Oberman, Heiko A. *Luther: Man Between God and the Devil*. Translated by Eileen Walliser-Schwarzbart. New York: Doubleday, 1992.

Otto, Rudolf. *The Idea of the Holy: An Inquiry into the Non-rational Factor in the Idea of the Divine and Its Relation to the Rational*. Translated by Das Heilige. Harmondsworth: Penguin, 1959.

Pascal, Blaise. *Pensées*. Translated by J. M. Cohen. Harmondsworth: Penguin, 1961.

Redfern, Walter D. *Puns* Oxford: Wiley-Blackwell, 1984.

Sweeney, John, and Bill Law. "Gene Find Casts Doubt on Double 'Cot Death' Murders." *The Observer*, July 15, 2001. http://www.guardian.co.uk/uk/2001/jul/15/johnsweeney.theobserver/print.

Taylor, Charles. *A Secular Age*. Boston: Belknap, 2007.

Tennyson, Charles. *Alfred Tennyson*. New York: Macmillan, 1949.

Troeltsch, Ernst. *Ernst Troeltsch: Writings on Theology and Religion*. Edited and translated by Robert Morgan and Michael Pye. Atlanta: John Knox, 1977.

Tutu, Desmond. "Desmond Tutu Peace Foundation." Accessed December 4, 2012. http://www.tutufoundation-usa-org/exhibitions.html.

Ward, Victoria. "Melvyn Bragg Attacks Richard Dawkins' 'Atheist Fundamentalism.'" *The Telegraph*, March 14, 2012. Accessed November 30, 2012. http://www.telegraph.co.uk/news/religion/9141951/Melvyn-Bragg-attacks-Richard-Dawkins-atheist-fundamentalism.html.

Bibliography

Williams, Rowan. *Dostoevsky: Language, Faith and Fiction: The Making of the Christian Imagination*. Waco, TX: Baylor University Press, 2008.

Wittgenstein, Ludwig. *On Certainty*. Edited by G. E. M. Anscombe and G. H. von Wright, translated by Denis Paul and G. E. M. Anscombe. Oxford: Blackwell, 1969.

Subject Index

Subject Index

Scripture Index

www.ingramcontent.com/pod-product-compliance
Lightning Source LLC
Chambersburg PA
CBHW030845090426
42737CB00009B/1118